Mennonite Women
of
LANCASTER COUNTY

D1716666

MENNONITE WOMEN of LANCASTER COUNTY

A story in photographs from 1855-1935

JOANNE HESS SIEGRIST

Good Books

Intercourse, PA 17534

Front Cover Photo:

Boiling Applebutter, 1902

A fall work day at the home of Ezra and Mary (Andrews) Mellinger, 127 Herr Road, near Ronks, Pennsylvania. Stirring the peeled apples in a copper kettle is "a home girl" known as "Aunt Martha." The young girl seated wearing a sunbonnet is Anna Andrews Mellinger. The grannie wearing a large white prayer veiling is Elizabeth (Hershey) Mellinger, Ezra's mother. Hostess Mary (Andrews) Mellinger is on the swing wearing a dark dress, while Ida (Rohrer) Mellinger sits on the right side of the swing. Visiting from Quincy, Illinois, and wearing a fancy white dress is Maud Rohrer (Homan) Allen, Ida's niece. Clarence Andrews Mellinger turns the apple peeler. Professional photographer Fannie Andrews, sister to the hostess, probably took this photograph.

Back Cover Photo:

Going Home by Honeysuckle Hill, 1916

Four young women walk near the Abram and Rebecca (Zimmerman) Diffenbach farm along the Old Philadelphia Pike and near the Mellinger Mennonite Meetinghouse along the Lincoln Highway. These are likely Diffenbach daughters with their friends. Photograph from the Diffenbach family collection.

Acknowledgements:

This book is possible because of the valuable assistance of many friends and colleagues. For their efforts and encouragement I am very grateful. Special thanks goes to historian John Ruth. As early as 1984 he fueled my vision for photography work and helped greatly in my documentation research.

Thank you to Carolyn Charles Wenger, Director of the Lancaster Mennonite Historical Society. Through the years she provided me with skills and resources. Because of her support I was able to bring over 2,000 documented prints into the Society's archives for the benefit of future generations. Additionally, she regularly encouraged me to develop a book about Mennonite women.

Thank you to Philip Ruth, photograph copy specialist who used his portable photographic system to make over 2,000 copy negatives from historic black-and-white photographs. He hand-reproduced most of the prints in this publication.

Finally I wish to extend my deep appreciation to Phyllis Pellman Good for fine editorial support, Dawn Ranck for excellent design, and Good Books for publishing this work. Several skillful mentors critiqued this collection at my request: Jean and Jim Druckenbrod, Kathryn N. Hess, Erin Kennedy, Kate Kooker, Frances and Donald B. Kraybill, Ivan and Mary Ellen Leaman, Don and Virginia Ranck, and Jill Snyder.

I want to also acknowledge the many persons who shared their family histories, stories, and/or photographs. (I apologize to anyone whom I have failed to name and to anyone whose photographs I have labeled incorrrectly.): Georgiane Bair, Henry Benner, Anna Blank, Alta Bomberger, Martha Jane and Roy Bomberger, Evelyn Becker, Arthur Brackbill, Rhoda Brandt, Milton Brubaker, Myrtle Bruckhart, Samuel Burkhart, Anna Mary Charles, Mildred Charles, Miriam Charles, Annie Deppeller, Vivian Denlinger, Naomi Denlinger, Margaret DeVerter, Sue Eaton, Arlene Eby, Esta Eby, Harold Eby, Helen Eby, Mildred Eby, Edward Foulke, Snavely Garber, Kathryn Geisinger, Helen Good, Anna Marie Groff, Earl Groff, Helen Groff, Elizabeth Grove, Dolores Harnish, Mary Harsh, Esther Heistand, Janet Heistand, Kathryn Herr, Mary Herr, Mary Ella Herr, Alice Hershey, Ann Hershey, Martha Hershey, Ruth Hershey, Alverna Hess, Clarke Hess, Ella Hess, Evelyn Hess, Helen Hess, Kathryn Hess, Myra Hess, Robert Hess, Marcy High, Grace Horning, Grace Horst, Elizabeth Hottenstein, Elizabeth Houser, Mary Lou Houser, Miriam Housman, Anna Mae Huber, Emily Kraybill, Esther Krantz, Martin Keen, Elizabeth Kreider, Anna Mae Lapp, Grace Landis, Rachael Landis, Rhoda Landis, Jean Larson, Anna Leaman, Anna H. Leaman, Carol Leaman, Ethel Leaman, Ivan D. Leaman, Ivan and Mary Ellen Leaman, Janet Leaman, Ruth Vogt Leaman, Lloyd and Miriam LeFever, Mary Lefever, Catherine Leatherman, Lois Lehman, Barbara Longenecker, Rebecca Longenecker, Grace Martin, Marilyn Martin, Richard Mellinger, Alta Miller, Anna Miller, Ann Miller, Barbara Miller, Harriet Miller, Naomi Miller, Dorothy Moseman, Mary Mosemann, Martha Myer, Doris Myers, Elizabeth Neff, Mabel Neff, Anna Mae Newcomer, Eileen Newcomer, John Nissley, Vera Nissley, Helen Nolt, Irene Nolt, Reba Nolt, Ellie Oberholtzer, Lorraine Petersheim, Arlene Reeser, Audrey Rohrer, Clarence Rohrer, Lilly Rohrer, Ruth Rohrer, Donna Siegrist, Mary Siegrist, Mary Elizabeth Siegrist, Christian Shenk, Clarence Shenk, Ann Smoker, Mary Anne Spangler, Mark and Ann Swarr, John and Florence Thomas, Diane Zimmerman Umble, Betty Warfel, Rhoda Weaver, Olive Weaver, Dorothy Weber, Alma Weidman, Chester Wenger, Grace Wenger, Ruth White, Martha Wissler, Jean Yunginger, Julia Zahn, and Elmer Zimmerman. This list does not include those persons who gave prints during the Photography Harvests for the Lancaster Mennonite Historical Society Archives.

My dearest thank you goes to my husband, Don, and our three sons—Brent, Philip, and Marc. They encouraged me to discover the faith walk of our people and enjoyed these stories with me. Now, by the grace of God, we're stronger persons for tomorrow.

Primary film composition by Philip Ruth

Design by Dawn J. Ranck

MENNONITE WOMEN OF LANCASTER COUNTY: A STORY IN PHOTOGRAPHS FROM 1855-1935
Copyright © 1996 by Good Books, Intercourse, Pennsylvania 17534
International Standard Book Number: 1-56148-205-6
Library of Congress Catalog Number:

Library of Congress Cataloging-in-Publication Data

Siegrist, Joanne Hess.
        Mennonite women of Lancaster County : a story in photographs from 1855-1935 / Joanne Hess Siegrist.
                p. cm.
        Includes bibliographical references.
        ISBN 1-56148-205-6
        1. Mennonite women--Pennsylvania--Lancaster County--History--19th century. 2. Mennonite women--Pennsylvania--Lancaster County--History--19th century. 3. Mennonite women--Pennsylvania--Lancaster County--Social life and customs. 4. Lancaster County (Pa.)--Church history--19th century. 5. Lancaster County (Pa.)--Church history--20th century. 6. Lancaster County (Pa.)--Social life and customs. I. Title.
BX8128.W64S54   1996
305.48'687'0974815--dc20

96-16703
CIP

Table of Contents

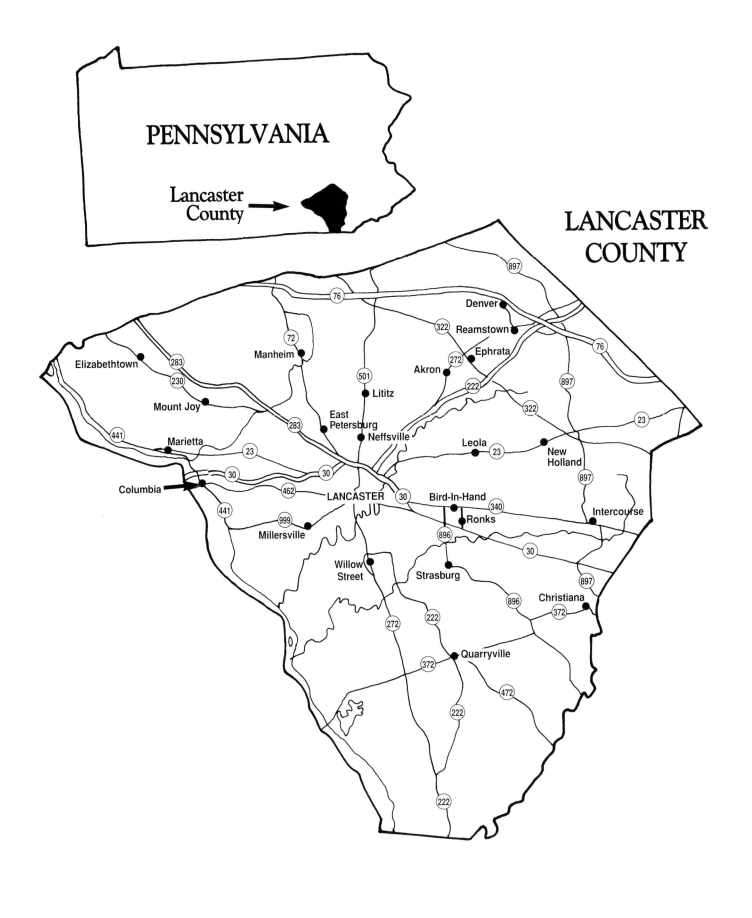

PENNSYLVANIA

Lancaster
County

LANCASTER
COUNTY

Denver

Reamstown

Ephrata

Manheim

Akron

Elizabethtown

Lititz

Mount Joy

East
Petersburg

Neffsville

Leola

New
Holland

Marietta

Columbia

Bird-In-Hand

Intercourse

LANCASTER

Ronks

Millersville

Willow
Street

Strasburg

Christiana

Quarryville

About The Photographs

This story and these photographs are set in the large Mennonite community of southeastern Pennsylvania, specifically Lancaster County. I began collecting historic photographs from this world in 1984 as I studied my own Lancaster County Mennonite family. My fascination grew, so that in the 1990s, I was concentrating my efforts on preserving classic photos and artifacts for the Lancaster Mennonite Historical Society. I felt an urgency to save the piles of forgotten photographs in attic boxes, cedar chests, and parlor drawers.

As a home economist my life work is the nurturing of family and community life. In the Mennonite community, that sense of belonging was transmitted carefully, but without a lot of fanfare, from one generation to another. Now, as a historian, I see how little was written about women, the substance of their lives, and the efforts they made to sustain values and character in their children, and their children.

My interest in Mennonite women and their stories began to take shape after I experienced several significant family losses. By 1968 I realized life was short and precious. I could not put off gathering family stories as a retirement project. I did little, however, until 1984, when our oldest son was in fifth grade. All the members of his class were asked to trace their roots back four generations. My husband and I did not know all those names, and few persons of our grandparents' generation remained to tell us our families' stories. At about the same time, I discovered drawers of unlabeled photographs. The stories that belonged to these pictures were all in the minds of a few older relatives, since they believed that most younger people were not interested in "that old stuff."

And so, my search began. I visited numerous elderly folks. Great Aunt Helen and I met fifteen times in 1984. From her razor-sharp mind came hours of stories, full of images. And then a friend taught me how to copy old pictures in my interviewees' homes without borrowing any prints. I began to see a story in each old photograph. Something wonderful happened as I sifted through family collections and stepped into the shoes of those long-gone mothers. I felt as though I had new eyes to understand family relationships. As the small prints were enlarged, I saw dimensions I had earlier missed. I was not the only one whose excitement grew. Relatives began to celebrate as together we held these priceless family heirlooms with new awareness.

Next I organized copies of the photographs in many different ring binders. As I learned additional facts from relatives across North America and Europe, I continually rearranged the stories. The gathering became an ongoing drama. I transferred some old photographs onto slides so that I could share them with family groups who wanted to hear and see their family stories at their reunions. The Hess reunion was the first group to see their history come alive through slides. Six other families eventually asked for their stories and pictures.

Now friends and relatives often request help with discovering and organizing their family stories. Sometimes classic photographs surface as a bonus to other findings. There is a growing call for publications and workshops on these themes. In 1993 I began a Harvesting Project to save, document, and organize significant heirloom photographs for the Lancaster Mennonite Historical Society. All these activities stemmed from a fifth grader's search in 1984.

I have learned that some families who hold the most heirlooms appreciate them the least. Many Lancaster Countians can trace at least seven different direct family lines back ten to twelve generations, all of whom have lived within Lancaster County. Once a frustrated Scots Irish friend announced to me, "You pacifist Mennonites have it so easy gathering your stories because so many of your people just stayed in Lancaster County, building big farm homesteads, while we Scots Irish fought your wars throughout the United States, losing many family ties."

Yes, some Lancaster County Mennonites are fortunate enough to easily trace their roots. I find that family stories and heirlooms fill an inner quest for defining beginnings and connections. They help provide identity and unity. Some hold a treasure of wonderful memories; others hold deep pain. Ancestral history is neither for personal credit nor deficit—it is only for learning.

Family stories are often like a bittersweet Old Testament story—they carry evidence of both weakness and strength. By learning family stories one can guard against the undesirable and build on the virtuous, since family traits and tendencies are often passed unawares from generation to generation.

A project such as this has numerous pitfalls—and benefits: the possibility of invading family privacy, the blessing of community, questions about the accuracy of detailed information, and always the limits of time for searching.

Despite that, I bring these stories so that all of us will find our way toward home. For those whose past is touched with pain, may this collection be a reminder that you can begin now to create positive memories for the next generation. May this book open new windows of understanding between the generations and between women and men. I hope, too, that readers and viewers will decide to organize and label their own personal family photographs, so that the next generation will more easily know their stories and roots.

How Scattered Photos Became a Collection

Gathering the Photographs and Their Stories

Nearly ninety-five percent of these photographs were found without any captions, labels, or written stories. The persons who were most able to help document the photo subjects were usually between seventy-five and ninety-five years old, so I needed to work as quickly as possible. Several times key sources died before I could complete gathering the data. I found additional information by reading family books and records in homes and churches, and at the Lancaster Mennonite Historical Society.

When I had gathered all I could find, I gave my proposed caption to the primary source for proofing. Sometimes I needed to change stories several times.

It was a new experience for many of these persons to see their words in print. Upon reflection, they remembered more or different information. Sometimes family members disagreed about their own family story. I sorted out what appeared to be the most authentic, and then added the disclaimer "probably" before the story.

From 1984-1996 I coordinated the harvest of more than 2,000 of the best known photographs about Mennonites of Lancaster County from over 300 households.

Security and Privacy

The full collection of photographs and their documented stories are housed at the Lancaster Mennonite Historical Society. I have agreed to protect the sources of this material for several reasons. With characteristic Mennonite modesty, some persons were concerned that they not "draw attention to themselves" nor receive "public attention." Others did not want to risk the possibility of "public calls." To further preserve family intimacy and trust, some captions are purposely brief, general, and without documentation. The acknowledgement section of this book lists the names of those who submitted prints or provided significant stories.

What Is the Scope of This Book?

The book focuses primarily on Mennonite women who were born before 1915. Each photograph contains at least one person who grew up in a Lancaster County Mennonite family or as an adult joined the Mennonite church in Lancaster County. The photographs come from almost all the bishop districts within the Lancaster Mennonite Conference; however, the distribution is not equal because residents of particular areas such as Lititz and Paradise seem to have taken many more photographs than those who lived elsewhere in the county.

At a few points I needed to choose between telling a more complete story or selecting the most choice photograph. I decided to tell the fuller story. Consequently, not all the photographs are of the highest quality.

All of the towns and villages included in the captions are in Lancaster County, Pennsylvania, so the state name is not repeated.

The Copying Process

Many of the photographs in this publication were made from copies rather than directly from the original prints. There were several reasons for this decision:

1.) Most persons did not want to lend their original prints. At our Photography Harvests, folks could bring their originals, watch them being photographed, and then take the prints home again the same day. Family pictures can be an extension of oneself, to be entrusted only to one's blood relatives.

2.) Although some folks with dusty, old, unlabeled attic prints began to value their photographs only after a historian showed appreciation for them, they were not prepared to loan originals to a printer.

3.) Many photographs were pasted in treasured heirloom albums which the owners did not want to leave their homes.

4.) The photographs came from several hundred households throughout Lancaster County and beyond. Gathering originals would have been a daunting, if not an impossible, task.

I continually felt the pressure of time, needing to gather photographs before they were sold, lost, or destroyed, along with the unwritten stories that belong with them. There is the matter of preserving the artifacts themselves. There is the equally important task of inspiring others to learn stories of their own past, and thereby lighting fires that warm family ties.

Joanne Hess Siegrist, 1996

An Overview of Lancaster Mennonite Women— Their Many Faces, Their Open Lives, Their Secret Selves

What went on in the lives and minds of Lancaster County Mennonite women who lived in the early twentieth century? Little remains about their day-to-day thoughts and feelings. Only a few women kept journals, composed long letters, or wrote family memory books. Diaries speak primarily of the weather and jobs; they highlight accomplishments, rather than personal thoughts or feelings, or reflections about relationships.

This much we know from hearing our grandmothers, mothers, aunts, and family friends speak. They regarded the Bible seriously. They highly prized the church, children, and cooking. They were women of the earth—practical, hardworking, and humble, filled with generosity, integrity, and faith.

Many women seemed to just work and work. One daughter recalls, "My mother moved like a chicken with its head cut off—going incessantly from one job to the next—seldom giving herself space to vent her feelings or express her inner thoughts. She always got a lot done. I loved when Mother cleaned my house. She got so much done. She just loved to work!" Most of these women were overburdened with the domestic demands of a large family and big farm. Journaling, diaries, and intimate conversations were far removed from their thinking or practice.

A lot of women did talk freely with each other, but they were insistently private about "in house" subjects. "In house" usually meant husband/wife or parent/child conflicts. In their social circles and family gatherings, women covered a wide range of issues and feelings, yet they usually upheld the "in house" standard. Some burned family diaries when their relatives died, believing that they were too private even to share with extended family and close friends.

While from our distance, these women may seem to have led plainly similar lives, pictures and their companion stories show a rich spread of experience. Some women placed a high value on living humbly, loving mercy, and serving others. They prayed a lot. When faced with difficulty, they "worked it off" by going to the garden or the barn. They could talk openly about their faith; they thought first and foremost about being written in the "Book of Life," rather than in "earthly" publications. The primary book in their homes was the Bible.

Some women were depressed, despondent, and dysfunctional, and they carried their anxieties privately. There were saintly healthy women who took their Christian faith so seriously that they shied away from church sewing circles for fear of gossiping as they sewed for relief projects. They visited homebound sick and elderly persons and read the Bible to them.

When a strict, stiff, plain dress code was enacted by the church at the end of the nineteenth century, some women rested in the security of the uniform conformity, while others wrestled deeply with wrenching bitterness. Family ties provided some women with emotional support and physical help, while others felt bound and boxed in by their families and their expectations.

This gathering of pictures is a people's view of history, based upon oral interviews about family memories. The several hundred persons who were interviewed revealed details, connections, and insights into what these pictures hold, and into the lives from which they have come.

Homestead Entrance, about 1904

Linden Dale Farm on Herr Road near Ronks was the homestead of Ezra and Mary (Andrews) Mellinger. Their daughter Anna, the girl in plain clothing, and two friends welcome Sunday guests.

Roadside Rest, about 1905

Landis Rohrer, Lizzie Diffenbach Martin (1889-
1984), Anna Lefever, and an unidentified driver sit on
the running board of a "tin Lizzie" along Horseshoe
Road in eastern Lancaster County. The young people
attended Mellinger and Stumptown Mennonite
churches.

The Clair Yunginger barn in the background
advertises Sinclair gas and motor oil, for which
Yunginger was paid an annual fee until the Depression.

Ascension Day, about 1912

Mennonite youth and neighbors gather in the meadow of hostess Helen Stauffer's family home near the Wabash Mill in Reamstown. The men played croquet while the women visited and prepared a cold lunch and hot supper.

In 1987, Alma Weidman (1896-1990), ninth woman from the left, recalled the supper menu they prepared: roasted chicken, mashed potatoes, filling, gravy, seasonal hot vegetables, pickles, chow chow, bread and butter, fresh and canned fruit, cracker pudding and tapioca, chocolate and white cakes, shoofly and coconut pies, foam and fudge candy, homemade ice cream, coffee, and meadow tea.

Early century hostessing was a creative undertaking that was long remembered!

Sunday Afternoon Play, about 1910

    Katie Leaman Hollinger wears a homespun calico apron as she relaxes from her chores and plays croquet with a friend from the Paradise Mennonite Church, Jason M. Eby (1890-1976). A ladder stands by a fruit tree, probably waiting for Monday morning pickers.

    A postcard print.

Ready for a Party,
about 1899

Ada (Risser) Metzler (1887-1947) of the Risser Mennonite farm community wears an elaborate hat. In keeping with a typical custom, she may have designed it herself. Beside her are house plants which were often put outside in the summer.

In 1907 Ada married John Erb Metzler. They farmed near Mount Joy, joined the Erisman Mennonite Church, and had four children.

Swing in Summertime, about 1898

At the Linden Dale Farm of Ezra and Mary (Andrews) Mellinger near Ronks. On July 16, 1924, a research skin specialist, Dr. Arthur F. McGinn of Providence, Rhode Island, visited Lancaster County. He concluded, "There are many things in Lancaster that please me, but the thing that made the most impression upon me was the Mennonite women with their becoming bonnets and their clear skins unmarred by cosmetics. I traveled all over the United States during the last twenty-five years, and I never found a group of women anywhere with such clean complexions."

The news clipping is from the Mary (Andrews) Mellinger collection.

Cooking, about 1915

Annie (Stauffer) Lefever (1875-1938) stirs supper while her husband, Enos Kreider Lefever (1872-1936), waits to eat at their home along Millport Road near Lancaster.

Annie and Enos' son Harry S. Lefever purchased a camera on April 21, 1915, according to his diary. This is one of Harry's first photographs.

Monday Wash, about 1915

Mary S. Lefever and her mother, Annie (Stauffer) Lefever (1895-1938), hang up wash along Millport Road near Lancaster.

There was order to this task. All similar clothing pieces were hung together—the white wash, the dark wash, towels, socks, and so on. The underwear was always hung on the back line, hidden from public view!

15

Getting Ready for Market, about 1915

Annie (Stauffer) Lefever and her daughter Ella,
beside the Lefever Greenhouse along Millport Road,
prepare rhubarb to sell at a street market on East King
Street in the city of Lancaster.

Doing Elderberries, about 1910

Three generations prepare berries for jelly at the Simon and Fanny Garber homestead, East Donegal Township. All are Garbers—Monroe, Helen, grandmother Susan, mother Fanny, aunt Anna, Suie, and aunt Kate.

Cultivating Tobacco, about 1914

Elizabeth (Landis) Bomberger (1895-1981) of Lititz guides the family mule.

Shelling Peas, about 1929

Rhoda Newcomer (1901-1972) on the front porch of the Newcomer farm homestead in Rapho Township. The family's pet dog, Sport, keeps her company.

Mellinger Mennonite Meetinghouse,
about 1915

Women entered by the door on the right while men entered by the door on the left. Sheds for horses stand on the far side. This church, built in 1884, was located along the Lincoln Highway, a few miles east of Lancaster.

The congregation first met in homes, possibly as early as 1717. The first meetinghouse was built in 1767 at this location. In 1996 the congregation had 375 active members who met in a building constructed in 1914 and renovated in 1988.

Relaxing on a Sunday Afternoon, about 1916

   Women and dolls line up after a large Sunday dinner. Blanche Shenk and Lizzie (Diffenbach) Martin, seated in the buggy, and their friends likely attended morning church services at the Mellinger Mennonite Meetinghouse. In the early years of the twentieth century, Sunday was Mennonites' primary day for socializing.

Risser Family Reunion, 1910

This third annual gathering took place Thursday, May 28, 1910, at the home of Nathaniel and Annie (Risser) Leaman, Front Street in Lititz. The Leamans served dinner and supper on the porch; roses gathered in the neighborhood add to the bounty on the tables.

Seventy-one year old Barbara (Breneman) Risser (1828-1924) is at the left center, the grannie with the white prayer covering tied under her chin. She is surrounded by three generations of kin. Her daughter, the hostess Annie (Risser) Leaman, sits at the head of the table. In honor of Mother Barbara the group sang, "Blest be the tie that binds." Barbara's youthful good humor was reportedly the life of the gathering.

Hayride from Strasburg, 1904

These sixteen young women, most from Mennonite farm families, met at Penn Square in Lancaster and took a trolley to the end of the line in Strasburg. Morris Kreider (1888-1958) and Ross Ranck (1890-1974) met them with this wagon. They took the women and their hats to the home of Abram and Susan (Kreider) Ranck, parents of Ross and Lydia Ranck, on Black Horse Road near Paradise. At some point the group stopped for this photograph, which was later printed as a postcard.

After a day of fun together, other male friends came to transport the women home.

By 1910 most of these women joined either Mellinger Mennonite Church or Stumptown Mennonite Church.

1904

23

Victim of a Train Accident, 1896

Barbara Buckwalter Hershey (1878-1896), above, of Black Horse Road near Paradise was killed at the Bird-In-Hand railroad crossing on July 26, 1896, while returning home from a Saturday night party at the home of John Musser of Witmer. A special high speed train on the Pennsylvania Railroad, carrying troops from the Lewistown encampment, struck the buggy carrying Barbara and her escort, Enos Barge of Refton. The couple were talking with friends in a buggy that was following them when the train suddenly came around a sharp curve. Barbara and the horse died instantly. Enos died in the hospital the next day.

Thousands attended the funerals, and the incident made a tremendous impression on young people in the Mennonite community. Young preachers from the Midwest began appealing to Lancaster County youth to stop sowing their wild oats and to join the church prior to marriage. Until then, the tradition was for persons to join the church after having several children, as late in life as ages thirty-five to forty. The parents of many of these young people would have followed that pattern.

The train tragedy greatly influenced the situation, so that hundreds of youth became church members. They exchanged their fancy Victorian clothing for an unprecedented, distinctive Mennonite dress style. The young people also adopted new social activities—hymn sings, Bible studies, and mission work.

A Gift Trip to Niagara Falls, 1897

Parents of thirteen children, Barbara (Buckwalter) Hershey (1840-1911) and Peter Eby Hershey (1839-1922), visit Niagara Falls with their youngest daughter, Martha (Hershey) Hoover (1876-1968), right. The Pennsylvania Railroad Company wanted to pay Peter Hershey some compensation for his daughter Barbara's death, but Peter refused to accept any money, not even to cover the funeral expenses. His steadfast reply was, "I will not accept any money for my child's blood." A year later Peter accepted a family pass from the railroad for a trip to Niagara Falls.

Two Views; One Woman, 1916 and 1918

In 1916 Bertha (Stauffer) Widders (1892-1958) wears her Saturday social outfit.

In 1918, as a new church member and engaged to be married, Bertha dresses in plain clothing. She made the change when she joined Hammer Creek Mennonite Church, where her parents were also members.

Bertha grew up on a farm near Lititz. At age twenty-six she married Reuben Widders from a nearby farming family.

A Wedding Portrait, 1899

Elam Landis Burkhart (1875-1946) of Mellinger Mennonite Church and Mattie Keener (1876-1947) of Strasburg Mennonite Church married on December 1, 1899. Mattie was one of the first Mennonite young women to wear the distinctive Mennonite plain garb. Her wedding dress has a pointed cape and an apron, and she wears a covering with its strings tied under her chin.

The Strasburg revivals of the 1890s greatly influenced this couple toward piety, simplicity, and separation from the world. Mattie stopped wearing her Victorian dresses, jewelry, fancy hats, curly hair arrangements, lace, and frills.

27

Lancaster Mennonite Women: The Tone of Their Lives

Early twentieth century Lancaster farms had qualities of paradise—families worked together from seedtime to harvest. Extended families and supportive neighbors surrounded many households. Children learned at a young age to help with significant family chores. And when they had free time, they found simple and creative ways to play with almost nothing.

Many women discovered great happiness and satisfaction in their lifelong commitment to marriage and raising a house full of children. They took strength from an earnest sincere faith in God, diligently reading the Bible, trying to live what they believed, possessing a living hope. Their lives of integrity often profoundly influenced others.

Quite a few women developed skills to make beauty out of a little. They created utilitarian art—quilts, braided rugs, wall hangings, and bureau scarves—from scraps such as feed bags, cord strings, and recycled clothing. Where others saw rags, they saw rugs. Where others saw rotten apples, they saw fresh applesauce. Where others saw remnants of yarn, they saw Christmas gifts.

Still others experienced great pain and scars from family and church patriarchs whose heavy-handed ways felt dictatorial and abusive. Some men forgot to put their hearts into their laws. In some families, the babies were born quite close; in some families, the number of children exceeded their parents' ability to care adequately for them and for themselves. Some women were crushed by neighborhood gossip; others fled from their people. A good number planted flowers everywhere, provided lots of laughter to lighten routine chores, and encouraged those who knew them with their stability, their strength, their security. They provided a rich blessing of heritage for those who followed them.

Mennonites and Early Photography

Throughout the 1800s, many Mennonites used the services of professional artists and photographers for formal portraits and photographs of special gatherings. The old prints can be found in various forms: engravings, oil paintings, watercolor prints, ambrotypes, daguerreotypes, cabinet photographs, and tintypes. By the late 1800s, some photographs were made into postcards or mounted onto large stiff backing.

Mennonites appear to have taken fewer photographs than some of their "English" neighbors. Ever thrifty, Mennonites may have deemed photography to have been a flagrant frill, although many Mennonite parlors held a fine photograph album. A few Mennonites even became professional photographers.

Before 1900, persons usually appear on photographs looking stolidly sober and without a trace of a smile. Slow speed film required that subjects hold absolutely still. Any slight movement made a blur. A subject could hold a straight face much longer than a smiling face. Children often appear scared because photographers warned them to sit like statues.

Major changes in photography occurred between 1918 and 1950. Fewer and poorer quality photographs appeared in Lancaster County Mennonite homes during this time. Events in the larger world contributed—the two World Wars, the Depression, and the availability of the home box camera. Another development affected Mennonite practice—some persons took a baptismal vow to avoid photographs and to burn their Victorian prints.

Photography Studio of Fannie Andrews,
about 1907

Sallie Foulke and her daughter Mareta (Foulke) Lichty (born 1905) sit in their sleigh in front of Fannie's Studio, 8-10 East Main Street, Strasburg.

A Fannie Andrews photograph.

Fannie Andrews,
about 1907

Daughter of Henry and Anna (Kreider) Andrews, Fannie Kreider (Andrews) Kreider Andreas (1864-1934) is Lancaster County's first known Mennonite female professional photographer. Fannie is also the earliest known *American* Mennonite female professional photographer. Family connections made it possible for her to enter the profession since her brother was a photographer. From 1902-1912 she photographed many persons and activities in the Strasburg community.

In March 1913, she left her family and friends in Lancaster County to marry Martin G. Andreas in Chicago. The newlyweds set up housekeeping and a new studio in Sterling, Illinois. Along with sixty wedding gifts from Lancaster County, Fannie took her large wicker studio chair to Illinois. Many of the photographs Fannie took show this large wicker chair.

Children Celebrate, about 1907

Newton G. Herr, a Mennonite farmer from along Herr Road near Strasburg, took his four children for a studio photograph by Fannie Andrews. Miriam sits in Fannie's wicker chair, while her brother Clarence leans on her knee. Bertha and Susan stand. Newton's first wife, Susan Mellinger, died in 1895, leaving him with twenty-two-month-old Miriam and ten-week-old Susan.

In 1898 Newton married Amanda Heller (1870-1932). They had three children—Bertha and Clarence on this photo and Emory, born in 1908. In 1994, one-hundred-year-old Miriam said, "My sister Susan lay very sick with pneumonia, and father promised when she got well we'd go to town for a family photograph. Mother Amanda sewed all the girls' outfits from a fine light green and white cotton plaid. First she made dresses for Susan and me. Just enough material was left over for Bertha's jumper. We all had to wear two petticoats so the daylight wouldn't show through. Oh, and I loved to use one of our four irons to press those petticoats."

Newlyweds Hand in Hand, 1855

The oldest known wedding photograph of Lancaster County Mennonites. Elizabeth Weidman (1835-1887) and Joseph Buckwalter (1832-1906) married on November 8, 1855. In keeping with the custom of their day, this couple probably was married in the home of a local Protestant minister and some days later traveled to Lancaster for a professional photographer to take a single pose print in a studio. Elizabeth and Joseph settled on a farm near Neffsville, joined East Petersburg Mennonite Church, and had six children.

Buckwalter's Anabaptist forefather, Francis Buckwalter, left Alsace in 1713, and by 1720 had purchased 650 acres in Pennsylvania.

Wedding, 1864

Henry F. Hostetter (1841-1911) and Anna B. Huber (1846-1919). Both Henry's and Anna's parents were members of Mennonite congregations. Henry and Anna joined East Petersburg Mennonite Church and began to dress plain when they became middle-aged.

34

Young Girl, about 1865

Mary (Rutt) Hoober (1859-1938) in a dress typical for children of Lancaster County Mennonites. Mary grew up and married Jacob Hoober. Together they reared eight children (Jacob, Emma, Harvey, John, Alta, Anna Mary, and two infants) on a farm near New Holland. They attended Groffdale Mennonite Church.

Mary (Rutt) Hoober is remembered by her great-great grandchildren as a wonderful pie maker, and some of those descendants still use her special recipes. In the early 1900s, Mary and Jacob's daughter Emma helped to start the Fresh Air Program for children of eastern U.S. cities.

Mother and Daughter, about 1862

Elizabeth (Mumma) Erb (1830-1907), wife of Samuel Bergey Erb (1825-1885), sits with the couple's first daughter, Elizabeth (Erb) Metzler (1860-1920). Samuel and Elizabeth Erb and their eight children attended a Mennonite church.

Mother Elizabeth wears a shawl-styled cape and a white lace covering, typical attire for older nineteenth century Protestant and Mennonite women.

According to oral history, this family from Drytown in western Lancaster County watched the burning of the Columbia Bridge in 1863 during the Civil War.

Sisters, 1908

Elizabeth (Brenneman) Eberly (1826-1919) and Ann (Brenneman) Hershey (1830-1915), daughters of Adam and Anna (Buckwalter) Brenneman, enjoy some golden hours of an "Indian summer" on October 3, 1908. They relax by crossing their usually busy hands. Perhaps they review the ways of the younger generations, talk of their health, and recall the past.

This photograph was taken by Barbara Leaman Moore (1884-1990), an early Mennonite photographer who used a square Kodak box camera. About 1905 Barbara started to develop her own prints, and many of her well documented photographs remain in good condition.

Trading Hats, about 1898

A gathering of Lititz area youth, some from
Mennonite homes, including Susan Bomberger Bucher
(1882-1985), back row, far right. Susan attended Erb
Mennonite Church with her family for the regular
services which were held one Sunday a month. On
other Sundays she went to parties with neighbors,
relatives, and church friends.

Susan's cousin Dillman R. Bomberger, a professional
photographer, took this photograph and then mounted
it on a finely designed matting.

Relaxing, about 1906

Little Annie Miller (born 1902), the youngest of eleven children, was the daughter of the well-known turn-of-the-century Mennonite photographer, John Kreider Miller (1859-1945), and Nannie (Engle) Miller. After attending Millersville Normal School, John married and set up a photography gallery in 1882 along Bainbridge Street in Elizabethtown. In 1885 after two children were born, the family moved to the southwest end of Maytown to the homestead of Jacob and Hettie Miller, John's parents. By 1902, eleven children had been born into the Miller family.

Between farming chores, John continued in his photography work throughout his lifetime, becoming an accomplished and recognized professional photographer. During the early 1900's John was visited on occasion by church elders, including deacon Abram Lutz of the Elizabethtown Mennonite Church. They requested that John take only personal family photographs and not make a profession out of pleasure, leisure, public photography. Miller understood his work differently than they and was thus expelled from the Mennonite church by 1908. In 1996, John's youngest child, Annie, age ninety-three, clearly recalled those photography debates.

39

Girl Crowd, 1915

Thirty-eight women and two men gather at the farm of Reuben and Susan Brubaker on Brubaker Valley Road, Elizabeth Township, in northern Lancaster County.

Nine young women work on embroidery projects for their hope chests.

Although only seven wear plain clothes, the majority of these young women eventually joined the Mennonite church.

Accomplished photographer Hannah Wissler, far left, pushes her trip-corded camera button to take this picture.

Socializing by the Barn Hill, about 1915

Edna Oberholtzer Landis, (1898-1982) with her friends from the Landis Valley community.

New Holland Youth, about 1920

Friends from the Weaverland Mennonite Church district try out a new camera during an outing at a Rutt farm in East Earl Township. An early telephone pole stands in the background.

John B. Landis Farm, about 1900

This homestead illustrates the prosperity, enterprise, and rewards of thrift so characteristic of many Lancaster County Mennonites at the turn of the century.

RESIDENCE AND FARM OF JOHN B. LANDIS, UPPER LEACOCK TP.

"Running Around"

Many Lancaster County Mennonite youth of the nineteenth century enjoyed a prosperity which was the fruit of their ancestors, who had labored for five to seven generations on the same soil. Their material well-being stood in sharp contrast to struggling Western frontier life, or the desperation and destitution suffered by thousands of poor European immigrants streaming past the Statue of Liberty and through Ellis Island during the same period. There is no comparison between these young Mennonite lives and those of southern slaves.

Mennonite young people worked hard and had little time for organized social life. Their main social activities took place on Sundays, at special farm sales, and, for young women, at Saturday afternoon girl crowds. Before the spiritual revivals began in 1896, there were no evening church services, and young people did not join the church until after marriage—often after parenting two or three children. Many single young people went to rowdy parties which often included alcohol, social impurities, secular singings, and pranks.

After the revivals of 1896 to 1910, many young people tamed their social behavior. They met on summer lawns, in autumn filled barns, in warm winter homes. A speaker often joined them to give a spiritual talk and read from the Bible.

Midwestern evangelists encouraged young people to join the Mennonite church before they married, and to adopt a distinctive, plain, and uniform Mennonite dress. At that time older Mennonite women wore a shawl-like cape and prayer covering, similar to the conservative styles of their Pennsylvania Dutch neighbors who belonged to other denominations. By the turn of the century, young Mennonite women began wearing a new, austere style of clothing and head covering. Eventually, the older women adopted this pattern as well.

Gradually, by the 1920s, a dress code developed, advocated as a means to be separate from the world. Mennonites of Lancaster needed a symbol to bind them together since their use of the German language was rapidly fading. In addition, many wanted to end the "worldliness" practiced by many of the youth. Mennonite historian John Ruth believes that from 1920 to 1950 was the most conservative period of uniform dress in Mennonite history.

Wealth, work, revival, and dress changes occupied many Lancaster County Mennonite youth at the beginning of the twentieth century.

Mount Joy Friends, about 1899

This get-together was probably hosted by Katie
(Nissly) Eby (1882-1958), seated in the center with the
black bow. The presence of Katie's two younger sisters,
Barbara and Anna, sitting on the far left side, indicate
that the event took place at the Nissly home. Their
parents, Levi and Lizzie Nissly, operated the Nissly Mill,
currently a part of the Donegal Mills Plantation and Inn
near Mount Joy.

Bridal Attendants, about 1898

After serving as wedding attendants for an unidentified couple from the Weaverland Mennonite community, these youth took a ride to the Strunk Photography Studio, 730 Penn Street in Reading, for this photograph. Many of these persons, as well as their offspring, became significant Mennonite church leaders: Sam Sensenig, Annie (Weaver) Miller, Adam Z. Martin, Emma (Weaver) Martin, John Martin, and Lydia (Martin) Hurst.

Charles Cousins, about 1873

Single young people from four Mennonite farm families of Manor Township visit a studio to be photographed.

Brubaker Sisters, about 1878

Three daughters of Christian and Mary (Hershey) Brubaker of Lancaster County. Barbara (Brubaker) Herr (1862-1942), Fannie (Brubaker) Lefever (1864-1934), and Mary (Brubaker) Buckwalter (1869-1961) dressed in elaborate garments which they probably sewed. Among their Mennonite farm family and friends, these Brubaker sisters were known for their fine, elegant sewing of Victorian clothing and hope chest pieces. Their Mennonite mother sent them to a fashionable sewing school in Lancaster.

Later these three joined the Mennonite church, and Fannie became the wife of Christian Lefever, a minister at the East Petersburg Mennonite Church.

Double Wedding Photograph, 1873

Brother and sister with spouses. These young persons eventually joined the church, and during the time when Mennonites became increasingly conservative in their lifestyles, they developed a belief against "graven images." Thus, there are no known photographs of these persons after this wedding photograph. Couple on left: Barbara Garber Nissley and John D. Herr married on November 13, 1873, farmed in Manor Township, and had six daughters.

Couple on right: Andrew Garber Nissley and Barbara Hess Bomberger married November 11, 1873, farmed the 1795 Nissley Homestead in Rapho Township, and had six children.

48

Six Sisters, 1896

Alice, Fanny, Barbara, Sadie, Mary, and Annie—six daughters of Barbara (Nissley) Herr and John D. Herr of Manor Township in the Sunday dresses which they wore regularly to Habecker Mennonite Church. In time, all six women joined the Mennonite church and began to wear plain clothing.

Upon marrying, each daughter received a dowry, including a Manor Township farm, at least eight quilts, and a piano!

A prominent tobacco farmer, their father hired farm help from the nearby town of Columbia. Concerned for the physical and spiritual health of his farmworkers, John D. Herr, with the help of interested parties in the Columbia area and surrounding congregations, dreamed of starting a new church in the community. On August 7, 1898, the Mountville Mennonite Church was dedicated.

The new church also accommodated older Mennonites who moved to town for their retirement years. John D. Herr served as an official founding trustee of the Mountville congregation, a building committee member, and the first superintendent when Sunday school classes began in 1906.

Courting Couples,
about 1892

These women—Lizzie
Leaman Rohrer (left)
and Lizzie Leaman Groff
(1874-1969) (right)—
were first cousins from
Bareville. Each was an
only child, and they
became as close as
sisters, celebrating a
double wedding in 1894.
Lizzie Rohrer married
Henry Hess Nolt; Lizzie
Groff married Aaron
Leaman Groff (1873-
1947).

After joining the
church and shedding
their "gay clothes,"
Aaron and Lizzie
became a long-term
deacon couple for
Stumptown Mennonite
Church.

A Full Corner, about 1899

The label attached to this photograph reads: "Home. Only party I ever had." The party's hostess was Minnie Nissley, seated in the front, wearing the light dress with the circular stripes around the neck.

Only four of her guests are identified: Christian N. Hershey (first row, first on left), Harry Flory (second row, third from left), Frances (Wolgemuth) Hershey (second row, fifth from left), and Katie (Nissly) Eby (third row, fifth from left).

Photograph from the collection of Minnie (Nissley) Stehman (1883-1951), daughter of Reuben and Annie (Wolgemuth) Nissley of Mount Joy, members of Kraybill Mennonite Church.

Friends, about 1924

Friends of Dorothy (Garber) Mosemann, a young Mennonite woman born in 1905 on an old Garber farm in West Donegal Township. (Dorothy is not on the picture.)

Girl Crowd, about 1915

Lacy dresses and plain dresses, probably all handmade by their wear-ers. Most of these young women came from Mennonite farm families. Five had already joined the church, including Miriam (Herr) Kreider of Strasburg who sits in the second row, second from the end on the right side.

Beautiful Woman; Beautiful Dress, about 1890

Lizzie Charles (Hostetter) Shenk (1877-1952), daughter of a Mennonite farm couple, wears a typical Victorian-styled dress which she sewed with intricate detail. She wore the dress to Saturday girl crowds and to Sunday services at Habecker Mennonite Church. A chain watch is tucked into her pocket.

In 1896 she married a West Hempfield man—Oliver H. Shenk. They both joined the Mennonite church after their marriage.

In 1920 they began Ridgeway Tours, the first tour group agency within Lancaster County. They served a broad clientele, personally escorting tours to Florida, California, Cuba, and Mexico.

Ocean Fashions,
about 1904

Fanny Diffenbach
(front left) of the
Mellinger Mennonite
Church and Christian
Rohrer (behind her) of
the Stumptown
Mennonite Church were
married in November,
1906. Not even ankles
showed in early
twentieth-century
swims.

Atlantic City, about 1918

Katie Brackbill, Mary Groff, Ruth Myer, Harry Lefever, and Landis Buckwalter spent the day swimming and going to the amusement park, just beyond the boardwalk.

The group is dressed in swimwear and beach caps typically worn by everyone at the beach in 1918. In fact, ocean police would arrest any female without long black wool stockings on the boardwalk!

Hotel Waitresses at Ocean Grove, 1915

These young women left their Mennonite farms and homes in the Elizabethtown community for summer employment at the shore. Typically, parents sent along an older single woman as a chaperone.

Ocean Grove, about 1916

Anna Charles and Ellen Landis of Lititz—the plain Mennonite women—take a sight-seeing ride along the ocean and beach. The New Jersey shore was a favorite vacation spot for Mennonite young people.

Atlantic City Boardwalk, about 1918

Dressed in their Sunday best to travel back home to Lancaster County are Landis Buckwalter and his girlfriend Ruth Myer.

Woman with Hidden Watch, about 1904

In keeping with the fashion of her day, Mary Rohrer Buckwalter (1889-1977) wears a watch cord around her neck with the watch tucked inside her cape dress.

On September 25, 1913 Mary married Henry H. Landis. They settled on the "Old Isaac Long Farm" near Landis Valley Mennonite Church and raised six children, including Elva who served more than fifty years in East Africa missions.

Standing Tall, 1909

A young member of the Weaverland Mennonite Church, Florence (Martin) Heller (1893-1972) poses in her new gingham cape dress which she probably made. Florence and two siblings were raised alone by their father, Eli M. Martin, after their mother, Lydia (Weaver) Martin (1868-1895), died three months following the birth of her third child.

Despite his additional parental responsibilities, the industrious Eli became one of the organizers of the New Holland Machine Company and the Enterprise Telephone Company at the turn of the century.

Florence married Harlan B. Heller in 1914. They settled near Stevens and became the parents of seven children.

Youth in the Parlor, about 1915

Mennonites of farm families from East Petersburg and Strasburg. Seated, left to right: Miriam (Herr) Kreider, Bessie (Peifer) Kreider, Susan (Herr) Hess, and Sue Rohrer. Standing, left to right: David Kreider, Amos Kreider, Paul Hess, Monroe Peifer, and photographer Enos Buckwalter.

Sunday Afternoon, 1914

These young women gather near the boat landing at Rocky Springs Park on the Conestoga River to feed the ducks. Helen (Snavely) Hess (born 1899) sits third from left. She remembers riding "Lady Gay," the steamboat, and the amusement rides.

During her adulthood Helen became a public school teacher, the wife of the deacon at Landis Valley Mennonite Church, and the mother of six children.

Summer Fun, 1923

ABC'ers cool off in the creek at the home farm of Mary Shearer in Rapho Township. The women include, from left to right Myra (Gamber) Good, Mary (Metzler) Frey, Barbara (Nissley) Miller, Fanny (Root) Forry, Mary (Hershey) Kreider, Mary (Heller) Landis, Irene (Brubaker) Landis, Sarah (Root) Landis, Anna Mae (Greider) Grove, and two children.

ABC stands for Always Busy Club, a woman's circle of fourteen members who met regularly from the 1920s through the 1980s.

Girl Crowd, about 1925

    Friends of Ethel (Barge) Leaman (1906-1988) and Anna (Barge) Leaman at a Mennonite home in Lancaster County, likely on a Saturday evening just before their dates stopped by to take them home.

Ephrata and Weaverland Girl Crowd, 1920s

Friends at the home of Elam and Lavina (Gingrich) Martin, Ephrata. A few years after this gathering, some of these Mennonite women became part of the Horning church, a more conservative Mennonite group that split from the Lancaster Conference. That church division did little to mar the warm friendships begun through girl crowds.

Heart to Heart Chat, about 1912

Ellen (Landis) Breneman and Kathryn (Leaman)
Swarr, both of Lititz.

A Mennonite Girl Crowd in Lititz, 1914

On July 11, 1914, Anna (Snyder) Erb hosted thirty-five young women in her home at 53 East Front Street, Lititz. Accomplished photographer Hannah Kreider Wissler (1884-1978), front row on left, takes the photograph as she sits with her friends and pushes the trip-corded camera button.

Most of these women lived within Warwick Township. The majority wear typical Victorian dresses, while seven wear plain dress, indicating that they have joined the Mennonite church.

Cooling Off, about 1899

    Under weeping willows near the barnyard is Harry B. Lefever, the first young man on the left, seated on a blanket surrounded by a group of unidentified friends. Harry was a son of the East Petersburg Mennonite Church minister, Christian Lefever, and Fannie (Brubaker) Lefever.

Weaverland Cousins, about 1907

Two sets of sisters. Left side, front to back: Lizzie (Sauder) Horning and Mary (Sauder) Musser, daughters of bishop John M. and Susanna Sauder who lived on the old Sauder homestead in East Earl Township. Right side, front to back: Fanny (Martin) Bowman and Mary Ann (Martin) Burkhart.

Picnic Along the Pequea Creek, about 1908

Young women from the Paradise Mennonite Church and its neighborhood. Anna Andrews Mellinger (1889-1947) sits at the far left at the head of the table.

A Wedding Shower, about 1908

Friends celebrating, likely near Mount Joy, include Ada Reist Kraybill, Mabel (Kready) Kraybill, Martha Bair, Anna (Reist) Weaver (1886-1971), and Mary (Reist) Greider (1888-1971). Anna and her sister Mary (front row, first on left) attended Kraybill Mennonite Church with their parents Eli and Fianna (Nissley) Reist.

Wedding Party, 1916

Elizabeth Landis and John Musser Bomberger married on November 9, 1916, at the bride's home, a Lititz Square mansion.

Their attendants were Paul Enck; Jacob Landis and his wife Bertha; Esther Erb, the flower girl; the bride Elizabeth, the groom John; Ellen Landis; Raymond Newcomer, the child; Harvey Metzler; Barbara Bomberger; and Paul Bomberger. Elizabeth made her wedding dress with the help of her mother. For their honeymoon, the couple took a train to Philadelphia and visited other eastern cities.

Reared by Mennonite families, the couple joined the Erb Mennonite Church soon after their marriage.

John's parents began Bomberger's Store of Elm, and the newlyweds worked at the store most of their lives.

Wedding Waitresses, 1915

Ira Leaman Hershey and Alice (Hershey) Hershey (1893-1994) were married on November 18, 1915, by minister Christian Brackbill.

These six Mennonite waitresses pose after the wedding meal, held at the farm home of the bride near Gordonville.

At the age of 100, Alice recalled her wedding reception menu: ham, little pastry shells filled with peas, mashed potatoes, fresh fruit salad with bananas, oranges, and pineapples, ice cream, and wedding cake.

The managing cook for the 150 guests was Margie Hershey. One-hundred-year old Alice quickly identified her waitresses, left to right: Susanna Rohrer, Esther (Kreider) Leaman, Edith (Patterson) Shultz, Margie Rohrer, Alta (Hershey) Fenninger, and Lizzie (Doutrick) Weaver.

Wedding Reception, May 31, 1938

Cook Annie (Kreider) Groff (1871-1941) stands by the porch during the mealtime blessing. Annie successfully managed several hundred wedding receptions throughout Lancaster County, and regularly cooked funeral meals and the annual meals held at Mellinger Mennonite Church for the ordained ministry of Lancaster Mennonite Conference and their wives.

On this day, in May, 1938, she served about 250 guests at the Abraham and Emma (Herr) Metzler farm homestead near Holtwood. The occasion was a double grooms' wedding reception for the Metzlers' sons Benjamin and Christian. The brothers married twin sisters, Ruth and Anna Walter. The separate brides' reception was hosted on another day by the brides' family. Another 250 guests were served at that event. The double wedding took place on April 6, 1938.

Cook Annie Groff, a member of Mellinger Mennonite Church and the mother of two children, was often assisted by her husband David. Many remember her special bread filling. Annie recorded her first wedding reception on November 14, 1918 and her last on February 15, 1941, the year of her death at seventy years of age.

In the 1920s, '30s, and '40s it was a custom among Lancaster County Mennonites for the bride's family and then the groom's family to each host a reception. It was common for 200 guests to attend each reception, for a total of 400 at both the bride's and groom's receptions. Wedding meals were large banquets, usually held at home.

During the 1950s, Mennonites began to use public restaurants, banquet facilities, and fire halls for their receptions. Over time, some larger Mennonite churches developed fellowship halls, thereby creating another option for wedding receptions.

Honeymooners at Niagara Falls, 1907

John Erb Metzler (1886-1939) and Ada (Risser) Metzler (1887-1947) boarded a train in Lancaster and headed for Niagara Falls, a typical honeymoon spot for early twentieth century newlyweds.

DLTL Circle in Wedding, 1925

The June 6, 1925, marriage of Mabel Burkhart and Frank Book. Some of Mabel's friends from the twelve-member friendship group, "DLTL—Do Little, Talk Lots" Circle, served as attendants: Ruth (Hess) Miller, Florence (Herr) Musser, and Elizabeth (Herr) Houser. Male attendants were George K. Book, James Rudy, and Harry F. Houser.

About eighty guests stood with the bridal party during the indoor ceremony because there were not enough chairs nor space to seat everyone. The day was very hot and some fainted in the absence of fans and air conditioners.

Honeymooner, 1933

Sitting on the car running board, Ethel (Metzler) Leaman (born 1912) prepares a roadside lunch as her husband Daniel takes the photograph. The newlyweds took a three week trip from Lancaster County to Florida.

At night their '28 Chevy became their bed. They left the back seat in Pennsylvania and carried a mattress with them, which they unrolled onto the car floor each night after chaining the front car seat onto the outside fender. Before the trip, Ethel made window curtains for their night-time privacy.

Contemplating,
about 1910

Amelia (Buckwalter)
Hess, 1895-1965, of
Manheim Township.

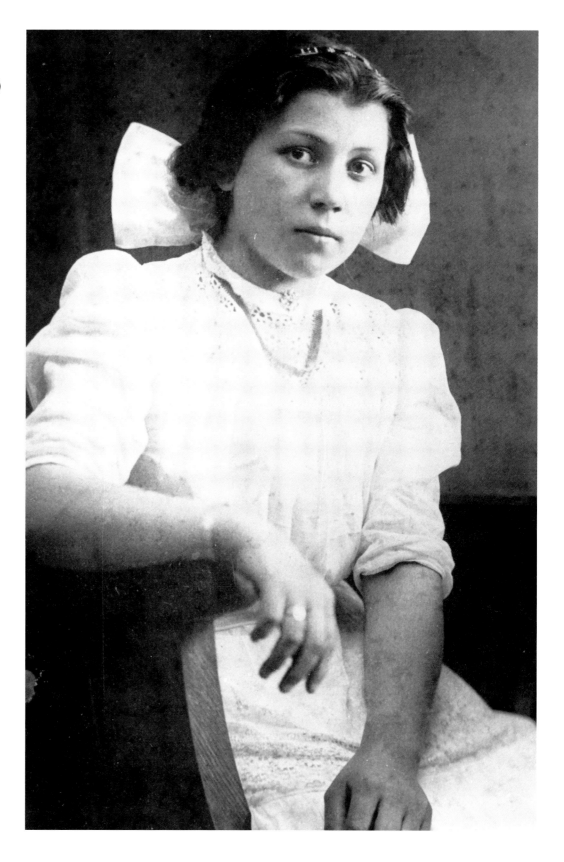

A Lover's Promise

When she was eighteen years old, Amelia (Buckwalter) Hess (1895-1965) began dating a local farmer, David Leaman Hess (1895-1965). Both Amelia and David were reared in Mennonite homes.

Soon afterwards, in 1915, lightning destroyed Amelia's family's barn. Certain that this was God's judgment expressed in heavenly fire, Amelia, her brother, and her sister joined the East Petersburg Mennonite Church. Their mother felt God's judgment, too. She had been sewing on Ascension Day, the day of the storm. She promised her family that she would never again sew on the holy day.

Amelia's farmer boyfriend, David, decided he didn't want "a plain girl," and so he discontinued their dating. Sometime during 1919-20, he became deathly ill with typhoid fever. During that time Amelia prayed for David's salvation and his love. She visited him, taking him chrysanthemums. She secretly promised God that for the rest of her life she would fast on the anniversary of the day of her visit, if David would marry her.

Amelia and David married on January 4, 1921, at the home of bishop Peter Nissley. She was twenty-six; he was twenty-seven. Amelia kept her fasting promise one day every year until her old age. After Amelia's death, David explained her fasting to a daughter who, through the years, had quietly observed her mother's practice. Finally the daughter learned the reason for it . . . Amelia's thanksgiving to God for providing her with a loving, caring husband.

Sunday Company, about 1908

The Harry Brubaker family of Lititz visits with newlyweds, Issac B. and Katie (Landis) Erb, the couple seated on the front steps.

Newlyweds usually married and honeymooned at the end of fall harvest days. After their wedding day, the new husband and wife each returned to the home of their parents until spring, when they set up housekeeping.

From fall until spring the newlyweds usually spent only weekends together when they visited friends to receive their wedding gifts. On those nights they usually slept together at the home of the bride's parents.

Motherhood and Children

For five generations—1850-1950—young Mennonite women dreamed similar dreams. To—

- Raise a big family—"Have your quiver full."

- Live in a fully furnished sprawling farmhouse with eight to ten rooms.

- Work hard from sun-up to sun-down—"Be a good steward."

- Houseclean every summer and fall—"Cleanliness is next to godliness."

- Raise a big vegetable garden, manicure several outdoor flower beds, and care for houseplants like African violets and ferns.

- Sew family clothing in the winter and use any scraps for quilts—"To waste is a sin."

- Keep the coming of a new baby secret until after its safe arrival.

- Expect house-help only after a new baby is born, and use that help for two to six weeks.

- Get advice only from family, especially honoring one's elders.

- Work side by side with one's children to teach them how to do homestead chores.

- Expect children to be courteous and to be seen and not heard in public.

- Respect God and the authority of one's husband.

- Entertain fifteen to thirty persons about once a month for Sunday dinner, using fine china, crystal goblets, silverware, and rich recipes handed down by relatives.

- Consider motherhood the highest of all callings.

Beautiful Lady, Beautiful Dress, 1861

Netted gloves, necklace, earrings, and floral brocade bedeck seventeen-year-old Mary (Good) Sensenig (1844-1882), daughter of Isaac and Mary Good. Soon after this photograph was taken, she became the second wife of John B. Sensenig. She mothered nine step-children and gave birth to eight children. The family joined the Mennonites, probably in the Weaverland District.

According to oral family history, Mary died at thirty-seven of "child bed fever," nine days after the birth of her daughter Barbara. She was buried in the immigrant Johannes Sensenig's cemetery near Hinkletown. The surviving newborn was cared for by the family. Her fourteen-year-old sister would bring milk from the springhouse, heat it on the woodstove, and give baby Barbara her nighttime feedings. The baby grew to adulthood, married, and had eleven children. This treasured photograph was her primary keepsake.

Mother and Child,
1907

Barbara (Leaman) Moore (1884-1990) of Lititz with her newborn son John.

Nursemaid with Mother, 1922

Nursemaid Sue holds the new baby, Paul, born on June 22, 1922. Just up from the traditional "ten days of bed rest," the baby's mother, Mary (Groff) Lefever, holds her twenty-two month-old son Elvin at their home along Millport Road near Lancaster.

The nursemaid assisted the doctor in the home delivery, and then helped Mary for two weeks—a typical practice in the 1920s.

Sue (Mowrey) Lefever served as nursemaid for many Mennonites of the Mellinger Mennonite Church and community; she also cared for her husband, Henry D. Lefever, and their seven children.

Rutt Family, about 1910

The Aaron Burkhart Rutt (1865-1947) and Elizabeth (Weaver) Rutt (1864-1925) family at their home near Honeybrook.

Both the number and spacing of Aaron's and Elizabeth's children were typical within the Lancaster County Mennonite community. Elizabeth was twenty-two years old when her first child was born and forty-three years old at the birth of her tenth and last child.

Aaron and Elizabeth made sure that all their children were taken to the shore to see the Atlantic Ocean at least once. In 1924 all of the family who were still living at home traveled to Niagara Falls.

Baby Annie, 1903

Annie rests in the shade while her mother Nannie Lizzie Miller works—probably cleaning the garden, doing laundry, preparing foods for winter storage, and manicuring the lawn for Sunday guests.

This carriage was used for most of John and Nannie Lizzie Miller's eleven children at their Maytown home.

Washing Up, about 1906

Annie (Miller) Deppeller (born 1902) sits on a washtub to inspect her toes. The youngest of eleven children, Annie was a favorite subject of her photographer father, John Kreider Miller of Maytown.

85

Mother's Love,
about 1904

Nannie Lizzie (Engle) Miller (1862-1937) with daughter Annie. Their old cookstove stands in the "out-kitchen" of their home in Maytown.

86

Hess Children, about 1902

Nettie, Norman, Minnie, and David dressed in finery, the clothes they regularly wore to attend services at Landis Valley Mennonite Church in Manheim Township. They lived with their parents, Ben and Lizzie (Leaman) Hess, on a beautiful farm near the little village of Oregon. Their mother, an expert seamstress, probably made all four sets of clothing. All wear black leather high-top shoes.

Sisters, about 1889

Anna (Nissly) Nissley (1885-1947) and Katie (Nissly) Eby (1882-1958), two of the seven children of Levi and Lizzie Lindemuth (Nissly) Nissly of East Donegal Township. Their father owned and operated Nissly Mills, currently part of the Donegal Mills Plantation near Mount Joy. The family attended Kraybill Mennonite Church.

Mennonites of Manor Township, about 1903

Young friends, before marriage and motherhood. By 1929, these four women had given birth to a total of twenty-eight children.

From left to right: Amelia (Charles) Charles (1881-1961) married local farm boy, John D. Charles who became a leading minister and teacher in Kansas. They had five children.

Martha (Landis) Charles (1884-1966) married John K. Charles who became bishop in the Manor District in 1918. They had three children.

Katie (Charles) Hess (1883-1979) married Jacob G. Hess who became minister at Millersville Mennonite Church in 1922. They became the parents of eight.

Leah (Martin) Lehman (1884-1954) married George E. Lehman, a local farmer who loved to lead singing at East Chestnut Street Mennonite Church. Leah and George had twelve children.

During their courtship days, the men who married these four women formed a quartet and sang at numerous Lancaster County gatherings of young people.

"Keep it up. It's good exercise!" about 1912

So stated the original caption on this photograph of Ellen (Landis) Breneman, shaking the rag carpet at her family's home near the Lititz Square.

New Phone, about 1919

Talking on her Independent telephone is Anna Catherine (Herr) Houser (1876-1945). The family lived in a new stone farmhouse built at historic Big Spring near Lampeter. The photograph was taken by Anna Catherine's oldest child, Harry Frank Houser, born November 2, 1901.

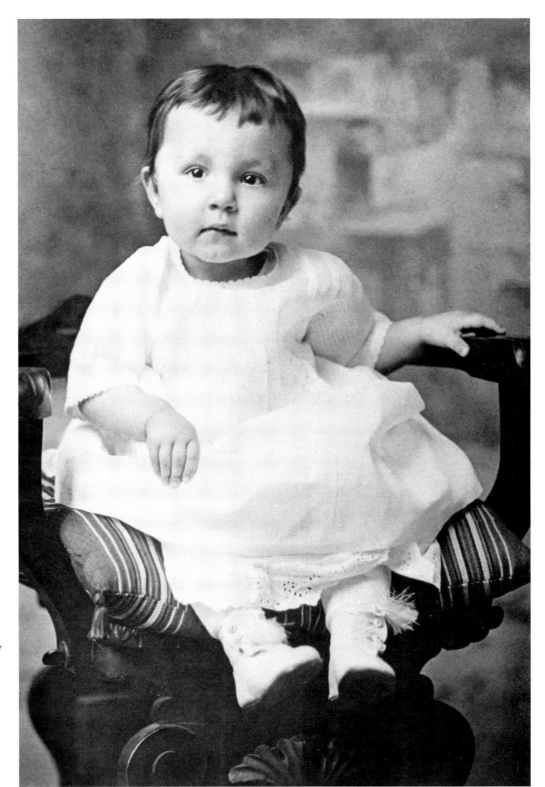

Thoughtful Child,
1918

Ruth Herr (Rohrer) Siegrist (1917-1990) grew up among Mennonite farm families near Millersville. She later became the mother of three sons (and mother-in-law of this book's author).

City Children of Lancaster, about 1910

Not all Mennonite families were farmers. Some lived in cities and towns. Holding china dolls are Florence Leaman and three Landis sisters: Anna Bella, Elsie, and Emma—all of Lancaster City.

Children of John and Susanna Siegrist, about 1922

John, Mary, Landis (seated in front), Jason, and Samuel were all born on a twenty-seven-acre farm along Beechdale Road near Bird-In-Hand.

Mary and Landis are wearing dresses made of the same fabric. Little boys wore dresses until they were toilet-trained.

Note the wooden water pump on the left.

A Shampoo, about 1906

Nannie Lizzie (Engle) Miller (1862-1937) gives her youngest daughter Annie a real scrub. Milk crocks dry on a bench nearby. The family lived on a farm near Maytown.

Sunday Visiting, about 1913

Elmer and Rebecca (Herr) Rohrer and their daughter
Kathryn (Rohrer) Herr (1911-1993) leave the farm of
Rudy Herr near the Millersville Normal School.

Leaman Farm House, about 1910

The Annie and Nathaniel Leaman home on Front Street in Lititz where they reared twelve children. The couple donated part of their farm land to the Lititz Mennonite Church, of which they were members, so the congregation could erect a church building.

Mother Annie sweeps the side porch, perhaps on a Saturday afternoon in preparation for Sunday company.

Harry Reist and Maria (Bomberger) Landis Family, about 1913

Emma, Ellen, father Harry Reist Landis, Jacob, mother Maria (Bomberger) Landis, Elizabeth, and Kathryn Landis. The oldest daughters are the two who are seated—Emma and Kathryn. Ellen eventually adopted a more fashionable Mennonite dress and attended Goshen College in Indiana. Elizabeth attended Linden Hall, a private high school for women in Lititz, and joined the Mennonite church soon after her marriage in 1916.

H. Reist and Maria had married on November 11, 1874 and began housekeeping during the spring of 1875 on a farm located at 763 West Lincoln Avenue in Lititz, given to them by Maria's parents, Jacob and Barbara (Hess) Bomberger.

From 1881-1895 Maria gave birth to seven children, five of whom lived to adulthood. The Landises were active members of the Erb Mennonite Church where H. Reist helped form the first Sunday School program.

The couple took their children on educational trips to places many Mennonites traditionally did not go, such as concerts, the circus, and historical museums.

In 1905 H. Reist built a large Victorian brick farmhouse at a nearby farm, 419 Arrowhead Drive, Lititz, for newlywed daughter Kathryn who had married Isaac Brubaker Erb.

In 1907 H. Reist and Maria, by then wealthy farm folk, had a farm equipment sale and moved to a mansion near Lititz Square for their retiring years. Maria spent much of her time quilting. She met an early death at age sixty-three because, as her family explains, "In 1917 she caught pneumonia as she sat by an open second floor window listening to an oration at the Lititz Square by her son Jacob, a graduate of Franklin and Marshall College."

Maytown Girls on Sleigh Ride, about 1906

Jacob K. Miller enjoyed entertaining neighborhood children. He boarded some students' horses while they studied at the Maytown High School. On this day he took the little girls of the town, including the daughters of John and Nannie Miller, for a ride in the winter snow. Here they stop at the town square with the Lutheran church in the background.

The Dowry of Maria (Brubacher) Reist, 1809-1887

Maria (Brubacher) Reist's dowry was first recorded in German by her father in *The Family Book of Jacob Brubacher*.

1828, March the 18, my daughter Maria Brubacher has this day entered into the married state with John Reist, and the following have I given to her as an out-fit to begin housekeeping.

Money for wedding clothes	$23.00
1-Saddle and Bridle	14.00
3-Beds with covers and Blankets	82.00
1-Drawer	18.00
1-Bureau	17.00
1-Kitchen Cupboard	18.50
1-Small Milk Cupboard	4.00
1-Bedstead	8.00
2-Bedsteads	7.00
3-Tables	11.75
Dough Tray and Butter Bok.	2.30
1-Wool wheel and Reel	5.25
11-Chairs	10.42
1-Coverlet	8.00
17-Cloths and other Table Cloths	21.00
13 Towels	5.00
12-Linen Bags	12.00
22-Yards Curtain Goods	5.50
12-lbs. Pewter ware	6.48
1-Large Copper Kettle	17.25
1-Spoon	18.00
Copper, Brass and Iron Ware	53.25
Other Ware	15.16
Tin Ware	13.80
Stone and Earthen Ware, 2-Bottles	19.92
1-Sett Iron Spoons	2.50
Stands	3.25
Bread and other Baskets	5.08
Hoes	1.00
2-Cows and 1 Heifer	43.00
4-Sheep and 4-Lambs	6.00
1-Horse	88.00
1-Pair Flax Handles	4.00
2-Pigs	5.00
	$574.41

Farm Life and Work

At the beginning of the twentieth century, most Lancaster County Mennonites lived on farms. Young and old worked together day after day, from Monday morning until Saturday evening. Sunday was the day for rest, worship, and visiting.

Children learned responsibility and work when they were very young. Their reward? The satisfaction that comes from doing a job well. Years later some of these children say, "I am so thankful my parents taught me to work. I still love to work!"

Garber Homestead, 1890

According to oral history, two persons in the center of the boat are probably Carrie (Weaver) Garber (1852-1918), fourth from left, and her husband, Benjamin L. Garber (1850-1932), second from right. The six others in the boat remain unidentified.

This farm is located southeast of Colebrook Road and Donegal Spring Road near Mount Joy. In 1741 William Penn's sons deeded 236 acres near Mountville to Christian Garber, the first known Garber immigrant to Lancaster County. Then in 1810, Christian's grandson Andrew Garber purchased this 258-acre tract in East Donegal Township between Kraybill Mennonite Church and Donegal Presbyterian Church.

Andrew built the barn shown on the left side in 1811. It was at this homestead where Benjamin L. Garber was born.

Pumping Water,
about 1900

Drawing water on the back porch of her parents' home is Anna (Herr) Herr (1881-1977), who married Ira Leaman Herr. The homestead is known as Herrbrook Farm. Its house was built in 1883 by Martin and Annie (Shenk) Herr.

Working Together, 1916

Mother Annie Gamber (Herr) Erb (1859-1917), far right, folds towels while other family members help with the Monday chores. Daughter Anna Mae darns socks, daughter Alice irons, and daughter-in-law Amanda scrubs clothes.

The Erb family lived on a farm along Stevens Street in Manheim and attended East Petersburg Mennonite Church.

Mother Annie, an expert quilter, quilted twelve months of the year. Often she delegated chores to her eleven children and then retreated to her quiet quilting room. The photo label reads, "Aunt Annie, Jack of all Trades, 1916."

Wash Day in Maytown, about 1897

Mother Nannie Lizzie (Engle) Miller (1862-1937) and grandmother Hettie Siegrist (Kreider) Miller (1835-1899) of Maytown scrub clothes by hand in wooden laundry tubs. They were at work early on a Monday morning.

103

Hoeing the Garden, about 1919

Esther E. Groff (1901-1978) hoes the garden in the company of neighbor boys Earl B. Groff, Elmer K. Denlinger, John K. Denlinger, and Lester D. Lefever—all Sunday school friends from Mellinger Mennonite Church. The activity takes place on the farm adjoining the church, the deacon Martin Mellinger Farm.

Esther, a single Mennonite woman, worked for many years at the Helm Candy Company. In her later years she became a domestic, doing ironing, cleaning, and lawn work.

Market Morning, about 1900

"Street markets" or "curb markets" were active in the city of Lancaster well into the twentieth century. Many Mennonite families left their farms before dawn. By sunrise their city market stands were filled with farm produce—fruits, vegetables, meats, and baked goods. These marketers visit stands along the steps to the county courthouse on East King Street.

Lancaster County
Court House,
Market Morning,
Lancaster, Pa.

Feeding Chickens, 1914

Three-year-old Mary watches chicks run up the ramp into the chicken house that stands by the old stone barn.

Mary was one of Ben and Ella (Snavely) Garber's seven children. The family lived along Bull Moose Road near Maytown and attended Bossler Mennonite Church.

Burning Trash, about 1907

Noah and Annie Miller at their home along Main Street in Maytown.

Whitewashing the Fence, 1920

Every spring the Lefever family of Millport Road, Lancaster, freshened up their homestead with limewater paint. The women limed the basement walls of the house while the boys painted the fence. On this day, Harry S. Lefever and a hired man, Elvin Denlinger, paint.

Barn Forebay, about 1912

Emily Lehman Kraybill (1898-1995) holds Dixie the horse, with her friends Elva, Elizabeth, and Edward at the Peter Kraybill farm, East Donegal Township.

Garber Homestead, about 1930

Cows graze near the home of Simon and Fannie (Eby) Garber of East Donegal Township. The Garbers raised their seven children on this farm—Suie, Helen, Norman, Henry, Clarence, John, and Monroe. Several became significant leaders within the Mennonite church.

Milkmaids, about 1923

The daughters of David and Katie (Nissly) Eby at their farm in East Donegal Township: Mildred kneels in front; holding buckets are Ruth, Vivian, Anna Mae, and Elizabeth, each ready to milk at least three cows. The young women milked every morning and evening, gathered eggs daily, and helped with other farm chores.

The family sold most of the milk to the Bachman Chocolate Factory in Mount Joy.

Eventually, three of the sisters graduated from college and entered teaching careers. The other two graduated from nursing school.

Milking the Cow, 1914

In the middle of the barnyard with no rope or stay, sixteen-year-old Elizabeth (Wiker) Sauder (1898-1976) does her daily chores on the farm of her parents, William and Mary Wiker of Quarryville.

Milk Delivery, about 1897

Levi Longenecker prepares to peddle bottled raw milk from the Amos and Hettie Sensenich farm, along Green Acre Road near Lititz, to customers in the nearby town. Dairy farmer Amos W. Sensenich (1862-1927) stands in front of the horse, while his two-year-old son Amos M. Sensenich (1895-1993) watches by the pump house where the milk was cooled in a cement trough before being bottled.

Harvesting Wheat, about 1925

Sunbonnet-clad mother of five children, Ida
(Weaver) Landis (1876-1962) rides the saddle horse
guiding the team, while her husband, Amos R. Landis
(1875-1971), cuts wheat with a binder.

The family lived on the Landis homestead, settled in
the early 1700s by immigrant Jacob Landis and located
between the Lincoln Highway and Old Philadelphia
Pike in East Lampeter Township. The plot is currently
the site of a large housing community.

Harvest Time, about 1910

Women and children gather to watch the summer grain harvest as the men thresh and bale. The threshing machine is on the left. The center elevator takes straw to the baler. After the straw was baled, two men wired the bales.

During harvest days the women supplied the field workers with cold beverages, such as vinegar punch and meadow tea, and prepared big, hearty meals. This threshing scene comes from the collection of Anna (Longenecker) Miller (1891-1974) of Salunga. Unfortunately the location identification and the persons' names are lost to history.

Watering a Tired Horse, about 1907

Annie and Noah Miller of Maytown at the pump trough.

Barn Raising, 1909

Forty-three workers at the farm of John B. Hertzler in Rapho Township. On July 27, 1909, a fine, large barn built just three years earlier was destroyed. Summer lightning ignited the barn near Salunga.

The property belonged to John S. Nissley and was farmed by his son-in-law, John B. Hertzler. The Hertzlers were threshing as the storm came up. Nissley had built the 1906 barn to replace a very old one along the Chiques Creek.

Neighbors Help, 1909

On July 29, 1909, two days after the barn fire, the neighbors rallied, bringing twenty-one teams of horses. They plowed twenty acres in one morning for John B. Hertzler after his tragic loss. Some farmers came with a team of three horses for one plow.

Early telephone poles are visible in the distance.

Barn Raising Cooks, 1909

Cooks of all ages gather on the front porch of the large farmhouse of John Buckwalter Hertzler (1856-1929) and Charlotte (Nissley) Hertzler (1862-1938), 1137 Newcomer Road near Mount Joy. Many of these women were relatives and neighbors of the Hertzlers. Some attended Chestnut Hill Mennonite Church.

In the center is John's and Charlotte's eldest daughter, Bertha (Hertzler) Bucher (1883-1962), holding her firstborn, Irene (Bucher) Nolt. Children enjoyed these frolics, while the adults found that cooperative efforts lightened work and boosted one's soul.

A Barn Raising Dinner, 1920

About 200 men eat after a morning of volunteer work at the Joseph and Bertha (Hertzler) Bucher farm near Lititz. At least a dozen women helped Bertha prepare and serve the meal.

Waitresses for a Barn Raising Meal, 1892

Roses and greens bedeck these young women and their neighbors as they pause before serving a sumptuous noon meal to the Christian F. and Annie (Landis) Charles family and friends, Garfield Road, Rapho Township.

Lightning burned the Charles' barn a few days earlier, and this was the day for the neighborhood barn raising frolic. Many of these waitresses attended Chestnut Hill Mennonite Church with their parents.

Feeding Chickens, about 1907

   Susan Bucher (1882-1985) and her sister-in-law,
Bertha (Hertzler) Bucher (1883-1962) do chores
together at the home of Joseph and Bertha (Hertzler)
Bucher of Lititz.

Barnyard Tour, 1909

Neighbors in East Earl: Luke Martin and his mother, Sue (Witmer) Martin; Emma (Kurtz) Martin; Clara (Martin) Metzler; Rebecca (Martin) Martin.

A Child with the Chickens, about 1914

Ella (Lefever) Weaver at work on her home farm along Millport Road near Lancaster.

"Sheeping Around the Buildings," about 1914

Without a machine to do the job, this young woman directs live weed-eaters to manicure around the family farm buildings of William and Mary Wiker of Quarryville. The woman is Elizabeth (Wiker) Sauder (1898-1976) with her cousin Benjamin Fager.

Snitzing Apples, about 1890

Grandmother Hettie Siegrist (Kreider) Miller (mother of two), daughter-in-law Nannie Lizzie (Engle) Miller (mother of eleven), and her sister-in-law Elizabeth Heller Miller (single). The three women lived and frequently worked side-by-side.

Baking Bread, about 1900

Anna (Haverstick)Rohrer (1853-1942), wife of Henry Stoner Buckwalter Rohrer, bakes bread at the mill house at Rohrer's Mill, east of Strasburg. These iron Dutch ovens still stand beside the mill in 1996.

Anna's brother-in-law, Christian Rohrer, built the Rohrer Mill in 1852.

Corn Husking Bee, about 1916

Getting ready for winter in East Earl Township.
Squatting: Stella Zimmerman, two unidentified persons,
Gertrude Stauffer, Kathryn (Hurst) Geisinger. Standing:
three unidentified persons.

Cutting Corn, 1918

Preparing sweet corn at the Elizabeth and Landis
Hershey farm next to the Hershey Mennonite Church
where Landis served as church deacon. Frequently,
food-processing was an extended family activity, and on
this day, Hershey relatives gathered: grandson Landis
Hershey next to his mother, Anna; an unidentified
neighbor girl; grandmother Elizabeth Hershey; an
unidentified child; and Ruth Hershey.

Harnessing Her Horse, 1920s

Mary (Lefever) Buckwalter (1900-1977) and her sister Ella with the family horse at their home along Millport Road, Lancaster.

Sunday Chores,
about 1912

Mary (Witmer) Landis (1900-1955), still dressed in "church clothes," feeds a calf at the farm of her parents, Hiram and Amanda (Reist) Witmer, near Erisman Mennonite Church, Manheim.

Stone Wall and Corn Shocks, about 1913

On the road between Terre Hill and East Earl, near the Conestoga Roller Mills. Kathryn Hurst (born 1905) said, "This wall was possibly built by a ball and chain prison gang, for I remember them building walls in this neighborhood. Preacher John Burkholder's home is on the left, while the home of my parents, Noah and Lydia (Martin) Hurst, stands hidden by the trees."

Ready for Fall Butchering, about 1925

Lydia (Hurst) Wenger holds the butcher knife next to Puncy the boar, anticipating the butchering which was to come the following week.

Children enjoyed butchering days because relatives and friends gathered to work, play, and eat lots of good food.

Peach Harvest, 1914

Mennonites and their neighbors gather on September 1, 1914 at C.B. Snyder's shed near Ephrata. Front row: unidentified person, Emma Rupp Snyder, unidentified person, unidentified person, Paul Stoner. Standing: unidentified Wealand, Martha Kreider Wissler, unidentified Drybread, unidentified Ridenbach, Edna Snyder Hess, Ida Rupp Snyder, Ida Stoner Hurst, Kate Snyder Stoner, Ed Wealand, unidentified Donmoyer, Charles Ridenbach, host Christian B. Snyder, unidentified person, Amos N. Landis, Isaac Ridenbach.

A Hannah Wissler photograph from the Historical Society of Cocalico Valley. Used by permission.

Snitzing Apples, about 1900

Nannie Lizzie Miller of
Maytown.

Weekly Washing of the Walks, about 1935

Charlotte (Hursh) Newcomer (1907-1948) cleans up in preparation for Sunday company. Her husband, Paul Revere Newcomer, is probably in the barn getting extra hay down, preparing for his day of rest. The couple attended the Chestnut Hill Mennonite Church.

Lititz Auction, 1907

February 18, 1907 along Arrowhead Drive near Lititz after many horses and carriages plowed through the muddy road. H. Reist and Maria Landis purchased this farm for their oldest newlywed daughter, Katie, and her husband Isaac B. Erb, and built this new farmhouse just like their own on nearby Doe Run Road.

On this day, tenant farmer John Smith sells his equipment.

Sledding, about 1910

Fannie (Groff) Peifer Stoner (born 1906) pulls her younger sister, Esther (Groff) Stoner Miller, on their family's farm along Creek Hill Road near Leola.

School and Studies

Mennonites of Lancaster County in the nineteenth century valued primary education. A number of Mennonite men served as school directors, and both men and women taught grades one through eight. Reviewing those early years, a former East Donegal Township teacher, Henry F. Garber (1888-1968), said, "The church and schoolhouse stood side by side. Christianity and education went hand in hand. The pastor often was the teacher and the Bible was one of the textbooks." When public schools developed, Mennonite men and women taught within the public school system as well.

In the early decades of the 1900s, most Lancaster County Mennonite children and youth had an eighth grade education which they received at a nearby one-room schoolhouse. Most walked a mile or two to school. Many of their classmates were from Mennonite farming families.

By the 1920s, about ten percent of Mennonite teenagers began to graduate from "in town" public high schools, while about one percent went on to college.

According to *The Mennonite Encyclopedia,* six high school-level academies were established by various Mennonite groups between 1893-1917. These schools, all of which were outside Pennsylvania, eventually evolved into colleges. Some Lancaster County Mennonite youth traveled to study at those schools. Although Mennonites of Lancaster County valued primary education for both boys and girls during the 1800s, they were less certain about the value of higher education, as it became more available at the beginning of the twentieth century.

One-Room Schoolhouse and Two Teachers, 1908

In the early years of the twentieth century, some Lancaster County public school teachers were young women and men from Mennonite families. Two are pictured above: Ada (Nissley) Garber (1887-1966) and Henry F. Garber (1888-1968), teachers at the Union School, East Donegal Township. On February 13, 1913, they married. Ada soon became busy mothering three children, born 1914, 1916, 1919, and serving as a pastor's wife. Henry fathered, farmed, pastored, and presided over Eastern Mennonite Missions from 1934-1956.

Goshen Students, about 1908

A friend reads to Ellen (Landis) Breneman (1890-1970) of Lititz. According to oral history, in 1908 Ellen boarded the train in Lancaster with her first roommate, Alta Mae Eby of Kinzers. They were headed to Indiana to finish high school. After two years of study, Ellen returned home. In 1917, upon the unexpected death of her mother, she cared for her father until his death in 1934. Then, after years of correspondence, she married her Goshen, Indiana sweetheart, Alpheus Breneman, and moved her household goods to his Ohio farm.

Ellen's first roommate, Alta, graduated from high school and college. She became an accomplished teacher, church worker, and wife of Paul Hess Erb, a longtime editor of the Mennonite church periodical, *Gospel Herald*.

Soudersburg School, about 1909

Sharing desks and studying together under the American flag are children of East Lampeter Township. The teacher, Miss Gorman, keeps order. First-grader Edith (Mellinger) Metzler Herr (1903-1987) sits in the center in a dark dress. Her eighth grade sister Mary Mellinger (1895-1970) is the only plain Mennonite student.

During evangelistic meetings by A. D. Wenger held at Paradise Mennonite Church on November 7-27, 1906, Mary, an eleven-year-old convert, recorded the nightly Bible texts and the names of the seventy-six converts from that revival.

Maypole Dance, about 1932

Twenty-two members of the Donegal Club House, wearing fancy spring dresses, dance for their family and friends who sit to the side. These young women, some from Mennonite families, include Ruth Eby, Mildred Eby, Ann Hossler, Bertha Erb, and Esther Lindemuth. They attended evening meetings sponsored by Mary Cameron and held in the building shown, formerly the Donegal Elementary School.

Young Women from Paradise, 1910

For two weeks in November, the public schools of Lancaster County closed so that teachers and friends could attend a Teachers' Institute in Lancaster.

After a morning of attending lectures, these six young women, none of whom were teachers, ate at the Crystal Restaurant on North Queen Street.

In September 1993, 100-year-old Alice (Hershey) Hershey (1893-1994) recalled the event. "We were all about eighteen and so silly. Each of us ate one dozen RAW oysters, a total of six dozen. That was all we ate.

"Next we went to a studio to be photographed. We kept laughing and laughing until our photographer said, 'Get serious or I won't photograph this group.' I can just remember that great day like it was yesterday.

"One word on the covering strings. You see how I tied mine in that little side bow while others put theirs down their back or to their front, and some wore black while some wore white. Today I still do not know the meaning of all that, but in those days we respected our church elders and did not question them. Now the next generation did ask questions and some took the strings off their coverings."

Front: Sue (Hershey) Hostetter, Elsie (Eby) Rutt, Ada (Hershey) Hershey. Back: Susanna Rohrer, Alice (Hershey) Hershey, and Anna (Hershey) Hershey. All six young women were Mennonites of the Paradise-Hershey Church District.

Graduation, 1902

As a sixteen-year-old, Barbara (Leaman) Moore (1884-1990), the oldest of twelve children, left her Mennonite family of Lititz for northern Indiana. She was going to attend Elkhart Institute, the post-high-school forerunner of Goshen (Indiana) College.

Barbara's parents, Nathaniel and Annie Leaman, greatly valued education and wanted Barbara to attend a Mennonite school of higher learning. Here she sits on the front row, the first woman on the left.

Upon graduation she returned to Lititz and worked as a secretary for the president of Animal Trap Company until she married Martin Arthur Moore in 1905.

Barbara became the mother of five children and lived to be 105 years old. Among her many positive, progressive activities, a highlight was her foundational effort to start Farm Women of Lancaster County on January 25, 1917. For many years Barbara and Florence (Moore) Brubaker visited Lancaster County women, encouraging them to try new homemaking skills.

Hikers, about 1932

Kathryn (Kauffman) Hostetter (1898-1990) and her husband, D. Ralph Hostetter (1896-1978), stand with their two daughters, Kathryn Ellen (born 1924) and Elizabeth Louise (born 1926), probably on the top of Limestone Hills.

In 1923 as a young married couple, Kathryn and D. Ralph left their Mennonite families of Lancaster County to teach at Eastern Mennonite School in Harrisonburg, Virginia. Ralph, a graduate of Franklin and Marshall College, Harvard University, and the University of Virginia, taught courses in biology, botany, ornithology, and geology until he retired in 1966. For more than forty years, Ralph maintained the D. R. Hostetter Museum of Natural History on the school's campus.

Kathryn worked full-time caring for their family. In their later years, Kathryn drove the family car while Ralph sat by her side, searching the land for birds and flowers. Every summer they returned to Pennsylvania to visit relatives.

140

Basketball Players, 1913

A plain Mennonite farm woman of West Donegal Township, Susie (Garber) Musser (born 1895) poses with her high school team at Elizabethtown College. From 1913-1915 Susie played basketball and took high school classes on the college campus.

Shenk Market Trunk Carrying Students to West Lampeter Vocational High School, about 1928

Helen (Hess) Miller and Mildred (Hess) Eby worked hard to go to school in 1926-1928. First they walked from their home farm along the Fruitville Pike to a trolley stop. Next they rode to Engleside where they met Clyde Shenk and his sister, Kathryn, who drove them in this market truck or a seven-seater Studebaker. Finally they arrived at Lampeter for a day of school!

In 1928 Lancaster County had several high schools; however, Lampeter Vocational High School was the first public vocational school. Some students traveled quite a distance to take agriculture and home economics courses. Lampeter families hosted boarding students.

Church Life and Faith

The Mennonite Church traces its beginnings to Switzerland in 1525. There, in the city of Zurich, four university students came to believe that one should be baptized when one makes a confession of faith, that baptism should symbolize a voluntary adult decision. This radical idea challenged the state church, as did several other convictions that this group came to hold, such as the separation of church and state, and a belief in nonresistance and the non-swearing of oaths. The group was contemptuously called "Anabaptists" (meaning to "baptize again"), and many died at the hands of the state church. The nickname "Mennonite" came from Menno Simons, a Dutch Catholic priest who became an Anabaptist within the movement in 1536 and who eventually became a significant leader.

In 1681 William Penn welcomed those seeking religious freedom to his "Penns Woods." From 1683-1770 some 3,000 Mennonites and Amish migrated to Pennsylvania. As they cleared the virgin forests, they were seeking to be quiet and peaceable people of the land after years of persecution.

The Mennonites of Lancaster County gathered regularly for Sunday worship, to hear preaching, and to sing songs from their time of martyrdom. By 1748 the Dunkers had printed the *Martyrs Mirror* at the Ephrata Cloister. Many households also had a family Bible from the Old World and a copy of the *Ausbund,* a book of German song texts.

Year by year families expanded and their homesteads became more developed. By the early 1800s some wealthy Mennonite men became involved in local politics and public education. Some young people were "sowing wild oats." Into this growing prosperity and settledness, revival began to come to some of the Mennonite churches of Lancaster County during the 1890s.

At the beginning of the twentieth century, there was a sort of "Great Awakening." Gospel songs were introduced, along with Sunday schools, evangelistic meetings, church membership for youth, distinctive Mennonite dress patterns, missionary efforts, publications such as the *Herald of Truth,* young people's meetings, and private Mennonite Bible schools and colleges. Churchwide institutions began to form during this time also. Mennonites were becoming more involved with the society in which they lived, while also creating an increasingly active church life of their own.

No. 16 Trolley, about 1916

These three young Mennonite women, friends of Lizzie (Diffenbach) Martin (1889-1984), stand at the trolley stop, probably near the Mellinger Mennonite Church, after a Saturday girl crowd gathering. Young Mennonite women often traveled ten to twenty miles by trolley for a Saturday party of thirty to ninety friends. Since the church forbade trolley travel on Sundays, persons traveled by horse and carriage to attend worship services.

Amanda Musselman, about 1890

A high-spirited young woman, Amanda went to parties, cake socials, and similar events with sons of some of the most affluent businesspersons in New Holland. One July evening in 1896 she joined a party at the home of friends near Witmer, east of Lancaster. Two of the young people at the party, Enos Barge and Barbara Hershey, had an accident on the way home. Their buggy was hit by a high-speed train at the Pennsylvania Railroad crossing in Bird-In-Hand. Barbara was killed instantly; Enos died in the hospital the next night. Thousands attended the funerals. The incident became a pivotal event among Mennonite young people in the Lancaster area.

That fall Amanda Musselman (1869-1940) was one of forty-three persons baptized at the Groffdale Mennonite Church. Describing the service, the *Herald of Truth* correspondent wrote in the November 15, 1896, issue, "The house was crowded to its utmost capacity, and many were unable to enter. Surely this was a touching scene. It tendered the heart of the sinner, and created joy in the heart of the saint and among the angels."

In 1898 Amanda went to the Chicago Home Mission to learn about city mission work. In the summer of 1899 she began mission work in Philadelphia with Mary Denlinger. By 1924, Amanda Musselman and Mary Denlinger were nearly synonymous with the Philadelphia Home Mission. As the primary long-term administrative team they served as Bible teachers, visitation workers, relief coordinators, placement persons for orphans, and sewing instructors.

In the early years of the 1900s Amanda gathered all the photographs of herself that she had given to her friends and burned those relics of her "worldly" years. Fortunately for history, her sister Katie kept this one picture, almost certainly without Amanda's knowledge. (This story is credited to A. Grace Wenger.)

Paradise Mennonite Church, about 1906

The congregation at Paradise Mennonite Church was deeply involved in early mission efforts by Lancaster Mennonites. The women of Paradise founded the first organized sewing circle of the Mennonite church in the United States.

Wedding Portrait of Amos Daniel (A.D.) Wenger (1867-1935) and Anna May Lehman (1878-1955), 1900

On March 10, 1900, A. D. Wenger arrived in Millersville, Pennsylvania after a fourteen-month trek around the world. On September 27, 1900, A. D. and Anna May Lehman were married at the farm homestead of Anna May's parents, bishop Daniel and Magdalena (Kendig) Lehman.

A. D. and Anna May met when he told travel stories at the Manor Township school where she taught.

On May 22, 1928, A. D. Wenger, the noted turn-of-the-century evangelist to Lancaster County, wrote, "There is a man who has a wife who has loved school all her life. She toils, scrubs, sews, and cooks and still finds time for books. Although past fifty years of age, she never tires of printed page. A student of Bible and sacred song, her school days glide smoothly along."

Ready for Church Membership, about 1905

Anna (Nissly) Nissley (1885-1947) poses in her typical Victorian dress. Born to Mennonite parents, Anna grew up within a close Mennonite farming community near Mount Joy. Just before her marriage on November 1, 1906, she joined the Kraybill Mennonite Church.

That event followed a revival meeting in February, 1906, led by Noah Mack at the Elizabethtown Mennonite Church, at which she and 132 other young people made their confessions of faith. After that, Anna began wearing the distinctive plain Mennonite garb of that time. Anna never altered her clothing patterns to more modern plain styles. She chose instead to always wear the pattern in which she was baptized, believing she received an extra blessing because of that choice.

Rock Point School, 1893

From 1878-1900, Lizzie and Levi Nissly's six children went to this public school for grades one through eight in East Donegal Township. In row two, the third girl is Anna (Nissly) Nissley, and in row four, the first girl is Katie (Nissly) Eby. Lizzie Nissly Nissly (1879-1894) stands on the back row, center left. When Lizzie died the next year at age fifteen of typhoid fever, her mother worried greatly about whether her innocent daughter found safety within the heavenly kingdom.

During the 1890s, some midwestern evangelists began telling Lancaster youth to put aside their partying and join the church early, rather than wait until they were married and had children, as was the earlier custom.

According to oral family history, one day an angel came to the Nissly kitchen, shut the door, and announced, "Daughter Lizzie is safe within God's kingdom." Mother Lizzie never worried again about her child.

Mission Work in India, about 1915

George J. Lapp (1879-1951) wears a hard hat and a white suit as he shows off two new cars he received from Mennonite friends from Lancaster County, Martin A. Moore (1884-1960) and Barbara (Leaman) Moore (1884-1990). George and his family served in India from 1905-1917 and from 1921-1945.

The Moores' passion for good vehicles led them to purchase and ship several cars to early Mennonite missionaries in India. On January 23, 1911, Martin and Barbara both drove their first car, the Premier. In 1913, eight years after their marriage, Martin, Barbara, and their two children left Lancaster County by train for a sightseeing trip to California. On their return trip they bought another car, a Jeffery, in Kenosha, Wisconsin, and drove it to their Lancaster County home. Family records show several photographs of other cars purchased by the Moores.

Mennonite Children's Home, 1911

The historic caption accompanying this photograph reads, "Dedication of Millersville Orphan's Home." A dedication service for the building was held May 31, 1911, at the Millersville Mennonite Meetinghouse. After the service, guests toured the new buildings located along Manor Avenue just west of the church.

Levi and Lydia Sauder became the first superintendent and matron team for the home. Over the next thirty years they served as "Papa" and Mama" to hundreds of children who lived there.

Tearing Strips for Rag Rugs, 1913

On a warm August day, the Paradise Mennonite Sewing Circle gathers at the Ezra and Mary (Andrews) Mellinger farm along Herr Road north of Strasburg, with these guests present: Fannie Hershey of Minnesota; Emma Ressler of Scottdale, Pennsylvania; Annie Hershey of Colorado; Lizzie Hess and her two daughters of Atlantic City.

In 1895 Lizzie Ressler of Scottdale wrote to her sister Annie Ressler of Paradise and asked if Lancaster County women would help sew for the poor in Philadelphia. The clothing would be distributed by the Needlework Guild of the Episcopal Church. The Paradise Mennonites agreed to help and began the first organized Mennonite sewing circle within the United States.

Paradise Sewing Circle, 1923

Mary (Andrews) Mellinger (1865-1927), a pioneer and leader, stands in front of the cutting table. A motto on the wall states, "Giving is Living." Early electric wiring hangs from the ceiling of the second-floor room.

From 1897-1918, each sewing circle in Lancaster County cut the clothing it was to make from bolts of fabric. During World War I, there was an overwhelming need for clothing in Europe, and so the Friends Service Committee of Philadelphia sent clothing pieces, cut and ready to be sewn together, to sewing circles in Lancaster County. In 1922 they discontinued this practice, and Mennonite mission leaders set up a room for cutting fabric above the Isaac Rutt Store in Paradise.

A Lancaster Conference Church, about 1920

Stauffer Mennonite Church near Hershey. During the summer, many Mennonite families attended all-day Sunday church meetings. Between services, families spread their packed meals on blankets and ate on the ground. Some older children usually stayed home for the day to do the essential farm chores, such as feeding and milking the cows.

Rohrer and Landis Gathering, 1911

Benjamin Siegrist Rohrer (1860-1932) and Mary (Landis) Rohrer (1859-1951) reared their four children on a farm along Creek Hill Road near Leola. The family attended Stumptown Mennonite Church. Here their grown children, Landis cousins, and friends gather.

According to a granddaughter, Margaret (Rohrer) DeVerter, "These folks are a fine example of warm family ties, even with different denominational beliefs. We enjoyed many wonderful gatherings. My father, John L. Rohrer, went to LaSalle University and lived in New York City. After graduating he worked for President Abraham Lincoln's son R. Todd Lincoln and attended a Presbyterian church where he met and later married a fashion designer, Margaret M. Gremli. My uncle Peter L. Rohrer worked at the Glick Plant Farm, served as the postman of Smoketown, married a Lancaster County Mennonite, and attended Stumptown Mennonite Church.

"The four Rohrer children are on this photograph. In 1917 my father and Peter began the P. L. Rohrer and Brother Seed Company. Folks often said, 'We've never seen brothers work so well together!'"

Hostess to the Lone Ranger, about 1934

Barbara (Ebersole) Brubaker (1892-1979) was an extremely good cook. Her husband, Jacob E. Brubaker (1897-1981), was proud of her cooking skills. Often on Sundays after services at East Chestnut Street Mennonite Church, Barbara entertained dinner guests in their home.

During the week, Jacob worked as a pattern maker for Hubley Toy Company of Lancaster, and occasionally Barbara hosted toy promotional guests. One evening Jacob called Barbara, requesting that she get ready for guests. To her surprise, he brought home the Lone Ranger. As the group prepared to eat, Jacob paused to explain that his family always prayed before eating. The Lone Ranger responded by saying that he wanted to remove his mask before prayer. Later he remarked that that was the first time he had ever taken off his mask in public.

Here Barbara and her youngest daughter, Barbara Esther, tend a well-loved flower garden.

Bird-In-Hand Train Station, about 1925

Fresh Air children wait to return to their city homes. From 1910 on, Lancaster County Mennonite families supported the Fresh Air program.

The tragic accident involving Enos Barge and Barbara Hershey took place near this station. That event sobered many Lancaster County youth and was the catalyst for a revival.

Wedding, 1916

Laura Lefever (1891-1974) and Bernard Kautz (1895-1978) pose after being married on July 26, 1916 by minister Sanford Landis of Mellinger Mennonite Church.

While single, both worked as hired hands at the Abram and Fanny Landis farm—Laura, a motherless child who needed a home, and Bernard, a Hungarian Jewish immigrant. After dating other persons, these two came back "home" to marry each other. Laura and Bernard both joined the Mennonite church after observing the lives of their employers and their friends.

The Landis family helped to provide a beautiful wedding and large reception for the couples' many friends. Additionally, the extended Landis family continued to relate closely to the Kautzes during their fifty-eight years of marriage.

Bound for the Shore, about 1929

From October 1928 through the 1980s, fourteen women called themselves the Merry Maids Circle and met regularly to socialize. Many such circles of twelve to fourteen women began meeting after 1900.

Here four of the fourteen Merry Maids stand with their suitcases during a train trip between Lancaster, Pennsylvania, and Ocean City, New Jersey: Irene (Bucher) Nolt, Anna (Herr) Kreider, Esther (Erb) Heistand, and Ruth (Rohrer) Herr. All wear a variation of the short fashionable sacque dress: one non-church member and three in plain dresses with long sacque-type capes. Many Mennonite women had an eye for fashion, despite the church's strict dress code.

Close Friends,
about 1910

Elta (Wolf) Miller, Carrie (Reitz) Myer, and Kathryn (Leaman) Swarr, all of the Mennonite community near Lititz. Elta became the first wife of Orie Miller, while Carrie's daughter Elta became the second wife of widower Orie Miller in 1960.

In 1920, Orie Miller traveled to Russia with Clayton Kratz to aid war-torn, suffering Ukrainian Mennonites. Soon afterwards, Orie helped to organize Mennonite Central Committee, a world relief organization with its headquarters in Akron, Pennsylvania.

"S. S. Tanganyika" to East Africa, 1936

Newlyweds J. Clyde Shenk (1911-1989) and Alta (Barge) Shenk (1912-1969) go on their first mission assignment under Eastern Mennonite Missions. While they dated, both felt called to missionary work.

Clyde, the only son in a family of three children, chose to leave a thriving Lancaster County farming opportunity. In 1935-1936 the couple studied at Eastern Mennonite School in Harrisonburg, Virginia. They married on August 14, 1935, and then, after a whirl of farewells, left for Tanganyika (now Tanzania) to serve a five-year mission term, which was extended to nine years, due to World War II.

Four Generations, about 1908

Generation 1: Ann (Grafft) Breneman (1826-1912), seated on right. Generation 2: Mary Ann (Breneman) Mylin, seated on left. Generation 3: Annie (Mylin) Shenk, standing. Generation 4: Susan (Shenk) Ebersole, center front.

The "Eternity" story on the facing page was told by Annie to Susan, who told it to her daughter Miriam, who wrote it in a book for her children and grandchildren. Five generations connected by one story.

162

How Long Is Eternity?

It was winter, and we could hear the cold wind howling outside as we huddled as close as we dared to the warm stovepipe coming up through Mother's sewing room from the stove in the long room below. Nyla and I were getting ready for bed and mother was sewing, as usual, making flannel nighties.

As I recall, it was an evening after Grandfather Ebersole had died, and I was thinking a lot about heaven and the word "eternity." And so I asked, "Mother, how long is eternity?"

Mother turned to me with a faraway look in her eyes and said, "I remember I asked my mother that same question a long time ago. She told me a little story that I never forgot. She said that I could pretend there is a very, very huge mountain, and every thousand years a little bird comes and takes a peck from the mountain and flies away again. When the mountain is all gone, eternity only begins!"

And I never forgot that story!

A childhood memory, written as a Christmas gift for her family by Miriam (Ebersole) Charles, daughter of Susan, the child in the center of the photograph on the facing page. Used by permission of the family.

The Orphan's Dress

Written by Fannie (Groff) Noll (1901-1987), an active member of the Chestnut Hill Mennonite Church and Sewing Circle, Columbia, Pennsylvania. Used by permission of the family.

Dear little dress for an orphan somewhere,
Lying so still on the sewing room chair,
The hands that cut you were saintly and true,
Perhaps not a mother, and yet mother too.
The sister who sewed you was jolly and sweet,
Her own borrowed girlie she dresses so neat.
She faced with great care each gather and seam,
Pulled out the last basting and tucked in a dream.
She held you up proudly and whispered a prayer.
Dear little dress for an orphan somewhere.

Dear little orphan for a little dress fair,
We wonder what color your eyes and your hair.
Your eyes dark and shiny or dreamy and blue,
Sweet lips full of laughter, and dimpled cheeks too.
Your hair so straight, vexing plain little girls,
Or dark, or golden and jumpy with curls.

But we wonder most if you've heard of the One
Who loved little children, and what He has done.
He called you, He blessed you, He died, He arose
That all little children have bread and have clothes.
The poor and naked and hungry and cold.
If we love Jesus and live in His fold,
Someday in Heaven, a white robe we'll wear,
Dear little orphan with a little dress fair.

Dear little dress for an orphan somewhere,
With others you lie on the sewing room chair.
Your gingham so fragrant, with charity's grace,
We love you much better than satin or lace.
Friends fold you and send you to hands waiting there,
Dear little dress for an orphan somewhere.

Family Outings

After working five and a half days each week, many Lancaster Mennonites looked forward to Saturday afternoons and Sundays. On Saturday afternoon Mother began to wind down, polished shoes, washed the front porch, and studied her Sunday School lesson. Pop swept the forebay and threw down extra hay for the cattle on Sunday. The young people took off for parties on many Saturday evenings.

At the beginning of the twentieth century, Lancaster County Mennonites usually attended church services every other Sunday. On the "off Sundays," they visited, especially with relatives and neighboring church friends. During the summer, some families took day trips to places like the Holtwood Dam or the Gettysburg Battlefield. They usually visited public places on Saturdays or holidays, rather than on Sundays.

A few families took the train to the ocean to spend a week. Farm chores, large families, and a spirit of frugality, however, kept many from vacationing beyond day trips. Whatever the chosen family outings, Monday morning meant the return to lots of hard work!

Pequea Creek, about 1904

    Overlooking the Herr and Mellinger farms along
Herr Road near Ronks. From the Mary (Andrews)
Mellinger collection.

Swinging Bridge on the Pequea, about 1904

Near the village of Paradise. From the Mary (Andrews) Mellinger collection.

Fishing, about 1904

Anna Andrews Mellinger (1889-1947) and her younger brother Clarence relax from farm work, probably on a Saturday afternoon.

Swimming in Little Chickies Creek, about 1895

Seven neighborhood girls and one boy wear old cotton dresses for a swim on the Eli and Fianna (Nissley) Reist Farm, Rapho Township. Three of the girls are daughters of Eli and Fianna: Mary (Reist) Nissley (1884-1964), front row, second from left; Anna (Reist) Weaver (1886-1971), second row, first on left; Mabel (Reist) Greider (1888-1971), second row, third from left.

Down by the Old Millstream, about 1918

Ada Kreider of Bird-In-Hand pushes her daughter Viola and a friend on a pulley swing, designed to fly over the water. Ada's younger daughter Miriam (Kreider) Steller (1905-1991) watches by the tree.

Atlantic City, 1916

Brothers Harry and Aaron Landis take a break from their adjoining Bird-In-Hand farms and enjoy a family vacation. Clyde, Harry, Mary, Bertha, Aaron, and Floyd Landis relax on the beach after jumping the waves.

Young Child, about 1896

Elsie (Leaman) Eby (1891-1965) of Bird-In-Hand wears her best going-away clothes, including black high-top shoes and tiny earrings. The photograph was taken by the Otto E. Weber Studio of 108 North Queen Street, Lancaster.

Elsie and her family attended Stumptown Mennonite Church and worked on their family farm along Mill Creek School Road. Her brother opened a racetrack on the farm with a half mile oval dirt track designed for bullet-shaped cars to go an average of seventy-five miles per hour. Along one side of the track were bleachers for 500-700 people.

Outing at Gettysburg, about 1915

Some Lancaster County Mennonites enjoyed day
trips to the Civil War site at Gettysburg. This group
includes Mary (Hess) Witmer, Ellen (Eby) Herr, Ira S.
Hess, John Newcomer, and his wife.

There were no public restrooms between Lancaster
and Gettysburg, so this group stopped at a stranger's
farmhouse and asked to use their outhouse and pump.
Nor were there public restaurants, so they packed
enough food for their day's trip.

Lunchtime En Route to Virginia, 1926

Mary (Groff) Lefever rests in the car with her baby Anna Elizabeth, while Mary (Lefever) Buckwalter, Ella Lefever, and Hilda Parmer eat a picnic lunch. The group traveled from Lancaster to Eastern Mennonite School's graduation services. Their cousin Mabel (Lefever) Gehman was graduating.

The driver and photographer was Harry S. Lefever (1897-1985).

Dinner in Cuba, about 1923

Oliver H. Shenk sits under the American and Cuban flags, while his wife Lizzie (Hostetter) Shenk stands by his side. Members of Rohrerstown Mennonite Church, the couple hosted this Lancaster County tour group in Havanna, Cuba, along with their son Christian, the tall man standing at the far end of the table.

A highlight of the trip to Cuba was when the Shenks' personal friend, Milton S. Hershey, took the tour group to his sugarcane and cocoa fields.

In 1920 Oliver H. Shenk, a real estate developer, founded Lancaster County's first tour group agency, which he named Ridgeway for the home from which he operated his business. Oliver codirected tours with his energetic, pleasant, plain wife, Lizzie. The Shenk family continues in the travel business as The Red Lion and Ridgeway Travel Companies.

Ready to Fly, about 1920

Grace Musselman stands ready to fly with her cousin Roy Musselman. Grace's sister Charity received a souvenir flight card from Musselman Air Service which says, "On September 16, 1920 Roy Musselman took her up 2,000 feet at a New Holland air strip."

Grace and Charity were daughters of George Musselman, a superintendent of the Sunday school at Stumptown Mennonite Church from 1900-1929. George did much Bible memory work during those twenty-nine years.

Touring Abroad, 1913

Anna (Ranck) Brackbill (1880-1963) at the Coliseum in Rome. As a single woman, Anna found time to travel, as well as to teach primary Sunday School classes for many years at Strasburg Mennonite Church.

On this trip, Anna was part of a group of forty-nine persons, the American Delegates' Tour to the World's Seventh Sunday School Convention in Zurich, Switzerland, July 8-July 15, 1913. Four Lancaster County Mennonites were delegates—Miss Anna N. Ranck, Mrs. Kate F. Mellinger, Mrs. Amanda (Book) Snavely, and her husband, Harry H. Snavely.

Harry, a respected superintendent of the Willow Street Mennonite Sunday School, was to lead the Lancaster County Sunday School Association, and he wanted training and resources. The Lancaster Countians made arrangements with Thos. Cook & Sons of Broadway, New York and left Boston on June 12, 1913 on the "S. S. Canopie" with 590 persons.

According to a preserved scrapbook and tour booklet, the Lancaster travelers made numerous stops before and after the convention in South America, Algiers, Egypt, Italy, Palestine, Greece, France, Germany, Holland, and England.

Before returning to America, the Snavely couple traveled to the Isle of Guernsey so they could bring home three Guernsey cows. In time, the Snavelys made ninety pounds of Guernsey butter weekly for their peddling route in Lancaster. Year around they charged sixty-five cents per pound.

The Lure of the West

Numerous Lancaster County Mennonite clans stayed within Lancaster County from generation to generation. From the early 1700s through the 1990s, ten, eleven, and twelve continuous generations of families have been at home there. These are people with surnames such as Brenneman, Burkhart, Buckwalter, Eby, Garber, Groff, Herr, Hess, Landis, Leaman, Longenecker, Martin, Nissley, Reist, Rohrer, and Siegrist.

A few frontier-spirited Mennonites forded rivers and streams for a new life beyond Lancaster County during the late 1700s and early 1800s. Some packed their Conestoga wagons to go to Ontario. After the 1840s some moved with the railroad. Other Lancaster County Mennonites went west for bigger and cheaper farms. Still others looked for a new environment to escape those whom they thought were too lax in their faith, where they could better preserve their Christian values. A few wanted to join mission efforts in other states, like Tennessee.

Of those who left Lancaster County, most maintained ties to home through correspondence and occasional visits. By the early 1900s a few Lancaster Countians "Mennonited-Their-Way" throughout the Midwest and on to California, visiting and staying with relatives and friends. Newlyweds sometimes traveled west to see relatives. In the late 1990s, many members of the Lancaster Mennonite Historical Society are from the West Coast, persons who want to keep connections to their Lancaster County Mennonite relatives.

The Hack, about 1906

In front of the Marietta Post Office. Twice a day—at
about 8 a.m. and 6 p.m.—Jacob K. Miller (born 1856)
of Maytown transported passengers to the Marietta
train station and carried mail from Maytown to the
Marietta Post Office. Miller's community service
benefitted this area of Lancaster County, where many
Mennonites lived. Those young women who moved to
the West depended on staying in touch with their
Lancaster County relatives through letters and
postcards.

Hess Family, 1918

A family in Kansas with roots in Lancaster County. Seated—mother Anna Hess, Helen, Vera, father Abraham Hess. Standing—Allen, Claude, Jennie, Abraham, Elmer, Grace, Ira, and Mary.

Lancaster newlyweds who homesteaded in Kansas, Anna Barbara Pfautz (1863-1940) and Abraham Lincoln Hess (1861-1921) married in 1883 in Lancaster County. In March 1884 they left their parents, friends, and congregation at Hammer Creek Mennonite Church to settle on a Kansas farm. Amos and Lizzie (Pfautz) Hess, brother and sister to Abe and Anna, traveled with them and settled on an adjoining farm.

In 1886 the Missouri Pacific Railroad acquired a right-of-way through their land, built a depot, laid tracks, and named the town "Hesston" after the two brothers.

Eleven children were born to Anna and Abe. The couple supported higher education for their family, so when a movement was started to open an institution of higher education for the Mennonite Church in the Middle West, they donated eighty acres of land for Hesston College and Bible School in 1909.

Five of Abraham's nine siblings left Lancaster County to settle in the midwestern states. Although separated by many miles, the Pennsylvania and midwestern Hess relatives continued to celebrate family reunions.

Couple in California, 1907

Ben and Frances Ann (Mowrer) Charles (1877-1962) await the birth of their first child at their newly established home. In 1907 the Charleses left Pennsylvania as newlyweds to live in San Bernardino County, California. Frances Ann worked at home, while Ben labored in the orange groves. They became part of the Upland Brethren in Christ congregation since there was no Mennonite church in the area. By 1913 they and their three children had returned to Lancaster County to settle among their Mennonite relatives.

An Independent Young Woman, about 1900

Colorful, spirited, energetic Anna (Nissley) Swartzentruber (1884-1975) took a nine-month trip to the West Coast in 1913 as as twenty-nine-year-old single woman. Leaving her Lancaster County farm family and her friends at Chestnut Hill Mennonite Church, she traveled alone by train and "Mennonited-her-way," visiting numerous relatives and church friends.

In her diary on May 16, 1914, she wrote: "I left the Upland, California home of W. J. Stowes with tear-dimmed eyes, feeling real sad because of the mutual benevolence I received there. Yet the joy of the Lord was flowing through me, which soothed me so peacefully." As she traveled along Yosemite Valley Annie wrote, "The scenery was such that even truth could not describe it." On June 30, 1914, she arrived at the Mount Joy train station, and then walked alone three miles to her parents' farm. There she was pleased to find everyone in good health.

Single until age fifty-four, Annie married twice widowed Benjamin Swartzentruber (1871-1960) of Upland, California in 1938. After a Lancaster County wedding, they left by train for New York City where they boarded a ship to go through the Panama Canal and on to California. Annie lived in California from 1936-1960 and often said those years were the happiest of her life.

Sightseeing in Chicago, 1909

Ella (Rohrer) Herr (1884-1980) stands alone near the Sears and Roebuck Department Store as her new husband, Jacob Hershey Herr (1887-1941), takes her photograph. After a home wedding on October 21, 1909 at the Rohrer family farm south of Strasburg, Ella and Jacob, a member of Willow Street Mennonite Church and a 1905 graduate of Franklin and Marshall College, escaped a rice shower when Harry Brackbill chauffeured them to the Lancaster train station in one of Lancaster County's first cars.

The honeymooners took a train to New York, Chicago, and Topeka, Kansas, visiting Niagara Falls, Chicago's Sears and Roebuck Department Store, and Kansas relatives.

Jacob wore a chest pocket which his mother made as a security measure for carrying his cash. His grandfather, J. Hoffman Hershey, head cashier for the Mount Joy Bank, taught the family safety precautions. Jacob also traveled with his own camera and took numerous photographs during the trip.

The newlyweds returned to Lancaster County where they began farming an old Herr homestead, originally part of the 1710 immigrant John Herr's tract. Ella and Jacob had three children: Arlene, Franklin, and Mary Ella.

The Farmers, 1924

Anna (Barge) Leaman (born 1909), age fifteen, and without any brothers, put on coveralls and cultivated Illinois fields with her father, Witmer Barge. Each had a team of horses. Back at the barn for a dinner break, they stand with Anna's younger sister, Elnora Mae.

Anna's parents left Lancaster County to farm in Sterling, Illinois from 1905 to 1925. They returned to Lancaster County for the last half of their lives.

As a petite eighty-six-year-old Anna said, "I remember this spring cultivating. Daddy and I did a sixty-four-acre field checkered-style. Oh, I loved that fieldwork!"

Sitting Room, about 1914

Photographer Fannie Andrews (1864-1934) left her Lancaster County Mennonite relatives to settle in the Midwest in March, 1913. She took with her many home furnishings, including her large wicker studio chair. Hoping not to be forgotten, and trying to bait visitors to come her way, Fannie mailed Pennsylvania relatives a well documented photograph book, including this postcard.

This print shows the interior of her new home at 608 Broadway, Sterling, Illinois. Fannie's relatives in Lancaster County had similar furnishings and decorating patterns; however, there are no known quality indoor prints of early twentieth century Lancaster County Mennonite homes.

Daughter with Elderly Mother, 1900

Christina (Neuhauser) Royer (1875-1967) and her mother, Catharine (Stoltzfus) Neuhauser (1833-1913). Catharine grew up in the eastern Lancaster County community of Gap. Then in 1872, her elderly parents, "Tennessee John" Stoltzfus and Catharine (Holly) Stoltzfus, left Lancaster County for Concord, Tennessee, accompanied by some of their married children, including Catharine and her husband.

In Concord this group started a new Amish Mennonite community and mission efforts.

Christina, the eighth of nine children of Catharine and Christian Blank Neuhauser, was born and reared near Concord, Tennessee. She, along with many cousins and their descendants, became outstanding leaders and educators.

Sisters Writing Letters, about 1910

Alice (Rohrer) Shaubach and Anna (Rohrer) Ranck (1894-1968) of Strasburg write to some of their many relatives in the Midwest.

Farewell to Relatives, 1909

Wearing large fancy hats, Edith, Isabel, and Anna Stoner (1893-1921) wait on July 27, 1909 for the Paradise Trolley to take them to the Lancaster Station to board a train to their Missouri homeland. Edith and Anna, chaperoned by their stepmother, Isabel, came to Pennsylvania to visit their Lancaster County Mennonite relatives, including their widowed grandmother, Maria (Buckwalter) Rohrer (1820-1912) of Strasburg.

From about 1865-1880, the Stoners' grandfather Christian Rohrer (1818-1897) went once a year to the Midwest to visit his eldest daughter, Emma (Rohrer) Homan (1849-1931) and her family. Christian traveled throughout the Midwest and found that the land was fertile and cheap, so he purchased 640 acres, two square miles in Missouri. He divided each square mile into two portions and built a house and barn on opposite corners. He then sent his younger daughters to live with their sister and her family for a year. The young women were to meet nice young men of the area. Christian Rohrer, their Lancaster County Mennonite father of ten children and the builder in 1852 of Rohrer's Mill, Strasburg, intended to give each couple a Missouri farm as a wedding gift.

Of the five daughters who visited, only one married a man from the Midwest and spent the remainder of her days there, namely Mary (Rohrer) Stoner (1857-1899). Two other daughters died at a young age, one never married, and one married and settled in Lancaster County. Christian Rohrer's will stated that the 640 Missouri acres were not to be sold as long as his daughters were living, so they would always be assured of income from the land.

Western and Eastern Relatives, 1917

The John and Amelia (Charles) Charles family of six traveled by train from Hesston, Kansas to Lancaster County to spend some time with their relatives. John went on to New York City for graduate work at Columbia University, while his wife and children stayed in Millersville with family. Here they gather with four generations of their extended family before saying good-bye and heading back to Hesston College. John had attended Millersville Normal School and Franklin and Marshall College before teaching science and serving as the first dean of Hesston College.

Three Sisters, about 1900

Coming together for a reunion are the daughters of Wayne Bare (1822-1912) and Mary (Landis) Bare (1825-1907)—Ida (Bare) Rohrer (1859-1943), Sarah (Bare) Kurtz (1852-1945), and Emma (Bare) Rohrer (1855-1944). Their grandfather Adam Bare (1789-1880) owned thirty-four acres of the Bare family tract, including the Tavernhouse, located in the family's namesake town of Bareville in eastern Lancaster County.

After Wayne married Mary Landis, he joined Stumptown Mennonite Church, the church of Mary's relatives. These three sisters attended Stumptown during their youth.

After their marriages, two of the sisters stayed among the Lancaster Mennonites, while Sarah and her husband Harry Kurtz left Pennsylvania about 1875 to farm near Topeka, Kansas. Sarah and her husband reared their seven children in the West; they lived in Inglewood, California for their closing years. Although separated by many miles, the Bare family stayed in close touch through correspondence and visits.

Visiting Relatives, 1909

Sarah (Bare) Kurtz (in the chair) and her daughter (front left) catch up on Pennsylvania news from Sarah's niece, Ella (Rohrer) Herr (1884-1980) (front right), a Lancaster County Mennonite bride whose honeymoon trip included this stop in Topeka, Kansas.

Quilting and the Arts

At the beginning of the twentieth century, Mennonite women of Lancaster County spent many hours doing elaborate, colorful needlework. Young women worked especially on their dowries.

With a frugality that was part of their spirituality, these women often created handwork out of remnants or half-used materials. They crocheted exquisite lace tablecloths from the cord string used to tie feed bags. They made hooked rugs using the unworn sections of old winter coats. They designed quilts with fabric from colorful feed bags found in the barn. Occasionally they did purchase fabric at a department store in Lancaster.

Fleisher's Knitting and Crocheting Manual, in its thirteenth edition published in 1915 by Fleisher Yarns of Philadelphia, provided many Lancaster County Mennonite women with crocheting and knitting patterns for afghans and pillows, blankets and coach covers, scarves and sweaters, slippers and socks, kimonos and negligees, baby and infant wear, mittens and gloves. *Clark's Designs for 100 Edges and Insertions* by Clark Thread Company, Newark, New Jersey, gave patterns for tatted handkerchief edges, guest towel insertions, laces for table runners, scalloped pillowcases, and laces for fancy doilies. Preschool children were given embroidery designs to encourage them to enjoy making beautiful things for their homes and to teach them the value of being occupied.

Many young women at the turn of the century learned to tailor coats and sew fine Victorian-styled dresses. But the revival movement that started in Lancaster in the 1890s greatly altered clothing patterns. Plain or fancy, most young women learned to sew dresses, shirts, men's suits, and winter coats.

Some women created wall pieces, such as show towels and embroidered genealogies. Framed paintings using oils or watercolors were rare.

Mary, An Unusually Able Quilter, 1860

Even though Mary (Sauder) Brubaker (1837-1910) lived into the twentieth century, this is the only known photograph of her. Mary, a farm daughter and the youngest of seven children, found her passion in quilting. She made numerous elaborate quilts, including a Rose Postage Stamp pieced with 13,689 three-quarter inch squares. Its matching pillow cases were each pieced with 1,152 squares.

At age thirty-three, Mary married for the first time, becoming the second wife of Abraham M. Brubaker, a local Mennonite farmer, schoolteacher, and druggist. At home in Goodville, they joined Weaverland Mennonite Church and became the parents of two children.

An Expert Quilter, 1948

Anna (Huber) Good (1876-1969) adds tiny stitches to a Grape Vine applique quilt. Anna quilted all her life; in fact, after rearing eight children, she became even more intent on quilting. Anna got up at 4:00 a.m. and quilted until 6:00 a.m. Then she made a large breakfast for her husband Daniel and sent him off to his market work. After doing a few cleanup chores, Anna returned to quilting. She quilted all day long until about 9:00 p.m., stopping only for meals.

Anna thought her retirement years were meant to be productive. She made forty-two quilts for her children. When she quilted for persons outside her family, she charged .015 cents per yard of thread that she used in the quilting.

Quilters, 1915

Mary S. Lefever, Kate Bealler, Elizabeth (Kreider) Lefever, and hostess Annie (Stauffer) Lefever quilt in the dining room of the Enos and Annie Lefever home along Millport Road near Lancaster.

On April 21, 1915, Enos' and Annie's son Harry S. Lefever bought his first camera and soon thereafter photographed his neighbor with these three generations of Lefevers—his sister Mary, his grandmother Elizabeth, and his mother Annie.

A month earlier, on March 27, 1915, Harry and his sister Mary were baptized with a group of sixty at the Mellinger Mennonite Church. Church membership did not halt Harry's photography; he continued taking fine pictures for many years.

Summertime, about 1910

A plain-suited gentleman watches an unidentified grandmother spin flax, while an elderly man reads, probably in his Bible. The photograph comes from a relative of bishop Peter Reist Nissley (1863-1921) of Mount Joy.

The attitude about the Bible held commonly by Mennonites of this time was: "God said it; I believe it; that settles it." They were not inclined to process cultural interpretations or ask questions of relevancy.

Children of John and Elizabeth (Stehman) Neff, 1908

The Neff family lived on a Manor Township farm and attended Millersville Mennonite Church. In 1994 Ruth White said, "My mother Annie, the oldest of these eleven, sewed all the girls' dresses by herself, and they each have a different decorative pattern." Seated, from left to right: Elizabeth, Ella, Bertha, Annie, Alice, Emma, Fannie. Standing, from left to right: Ada, Henry, John, and Mary. All eleven children became Mennonites and lifelong residents of Lancaster County, except Ada who married Daniel W. Lehman, a long-term professor at Eastern Mennonite College, Harrisonburg, Virginia.

Accomplished Seamstress,
about 1880

Lizzie (Leaman) Hess (1864-1944) probably made this decorative dress of polished cotton and velveteen that she is wearing. The dress and its story have been lost with time. What is known is that Lizzie and her three sisters made elaborately sewn pieces.

Lizzie is dressed as a typical young woman from a Mennonite family. When she was thirty-six and the mother of three children—Minnie, Nettie, and David—she joined Landis Valley Mennonite Church with her husband, Benjamin H. Hess. They both changed to wearing plain attire. Later Lizzie and Benjamin had a fourth child, Norman.

Sewing Club, about 1919

Home from Goshen College, Ellen (Landis) Breneman (1890-1970) of Lititz sits on the left beside the treadle sewing machine. She, along with many of her Mennonite friends, took professional sewing lessons, often in Lancaster City, to learn exquisite, detailed Victorian sewing.

Note the typical coat hook railing, Victorian wall covering, hanging calendar, and the dark painted woodwork.

Canadian Pen Pals Visit Lancaster, 1920s

During the late 1800s, some Lancaster Mennonites honeymooned in Kitchener, Ontario. Many continued friendships with Canadian Mennonites. In time, some of their children formed pen pal circle letters.

On this day, Gladys Snyder of Canada visits in Pennsylvania, seated on the far right with her cousins. She was a long-time pen pal of Barbara (Nissley) Miller of Landisville. Three girls knit while the other two relax on a summer day.

Quilting Team, about 1935

A traveling quilting team work this day at the home of Paul Revere Newcomer, Mount Joy. Two additional helpers include Paul's single sisters, back right.

After the Newcomer quilts were completed, these women went to other Mennonite homes near East Petersburg and Landisville. The group includes: Kate (Stauffer) Eby, Lizzie Ann (Kauffman) Kreider, Mary Kauffman, Barbara Kauffman, Lilly Kauffman, Lizzie Groff, plus Anna Mary and Rhoda Newcomer.

Violin Player,
1926-1928

Upon returning to Pennsylvania and moving to a rental property on Creek Hill Road near Leola, Anna (Barge) Leaman (born 1909) began taking violin lessons from a Mr. Everett. He was an unusually talented Russian Mennonite immigrant who taught over fifty local children piano and violin. Anna borrowed her violin from a cousin.

Sisters, about 1905

Lizzie and Vera Landis pose in their Sunday dresses next to an old spinning wheel. Their parents were Mennonites from the Ephrata community.

ABC Circle, 1923

These young women prepare hope chest items— weaving baskets and embroidering bureau scarves—at the Root twins' home near East Petersburg.

This group, known as the "ABC"-ers ("Always Busy Circle"), got together regularly for more than fifty years.

Summertime Relaxation, about 1935

Minnie (Nissley) Stehman (1883-1951) and her husband John Nissley Stehman (1880-1968). Minnie was a self-taught architect who designed at least six homes plus an apartment complex in the Manheim community, while her husband built the homes. Here they relax at their Mount Gretna summer cottage.

Members of the East Petersburg Mennonite Church, they had two children: Anna Mae (Stehman) Housman (1904-1991) and J. Nissley Stehman. Anna Mae also became an accomplished architect, as well as a building contractor for twenty-five houses within Lancaster County, some for executives of Armstrong World Industries.

Five-Year-Old, 1907

At the age of five, Mary (Weaver) Harsh (1902-1994) pieced a quilt with family remnant prints. Her grandmother Mary Ann (Burkholder) Weaver (1848-1918) cut out the patches and made pencil lines so that Mary could hand-stitch the patches together. Her mother, Annie (Good) Weaver (1884-1946), quilted it.

In 1907 the project was recognized in the *New Holland Clarion* (see below). The newsclipping was saved in a family Bible for many years, from 1907-1994. The well preserved quilt is now a family heirloom.

Busy at Five.

Mary Edna, daughter of Mr. and Mrs. Mahlon S. Weaver, of Lancaster, formerly of East Earl, has accomplished a remarkable feat for one of such tender years. Tho she is not quite five years of age she has pieced a quilt of seventy-two pieces, each piece containing four patches. Everything relative to the work she has done herself and in a neat manner. It is doubtful if another child in the county of the same age has accomplished such a piece of work.

Older Years and Reunions

At the close of the nineteenth and the beginning of the twentieth centuries, older Lancaster County Mennonites usually lived next to one of their married children. If they had an unmarried daughter, it was customary for her to live with her aging parents and care for them.

While the farm offered many chores for aging parents, those in their retirement years also occupied themselves with telling stories to the younger generations and reminiscing with relatives, often on the front porch.

About 1900, large extended family reunions became common, both within and outside the Mennonite community. Since many Mennonite families had lived in Lancaster County from the early 1700s, clans began listing their genealogies and histories. Scores of relatives would gather at a significant family homestead. Sometimes a midwestern or West Coast family representative would attend. A guest photographer and news writer often documented the grand occasion.

Eby Reunion, 1912

The first official reunion for the Henry N. Eby family, held in a grove in the meadow at the Henry and Anna Eby farm near Salunga.

Grandma Elizabeth (Hostetter) Eby and Grandma Hettie Reist sit on rocking chairs in the farm meadow. A car seat lies beside the tablecloth for anyone who prefers not to sit on the ground

Other guests include Annie (Reist) Eby and her son Charles Eby, and Elizabeth (Eby) Brenneman next to the rocking-chair grandmothers. David and Katie (Nissly) Eby and their three eldest daughters, Anna Mae, Ruth, and Elizabeth, sit on the far right. Hand towels hang from the tree trunk.

Family members arrived between nine-thirty and ten in the morning, bringing their picnic lunches, lemon juice and sugar to add to the ten-gallon crock of lemonade, and cakes to share with the whole gathering.

Before eating, the group sang together, listened to scripture reading, and offered prayers of thanks. After the meal, they sang, visited, fished, played quoits, and swam in the Big Chiques Creek. At four-thirty, they ended the event with ice cream.

The Eby reunions continued annually until 1942, when the family took a two-year break because of gasoline restrictions during World War II.

The gatherings resumed, then, meeting nearly every year at a variety of community parks, rather than at the Eby homestead.

50th Wedding Anniversary, 1935

Rudolph Landis Herr (1859-1941) and Susan (Gingrich) Herr (1865-1945) of Millersville share a quiet seasoned love during a celebration at their home with their children and grandchildren.

At the turn of the century this couple farmed and reared their three children on the current site of Millersville University's Student Center. (Rudolph's brother Christian managed Herr's Ice Plant along the Columbia Pike near Lancaster.) Rudolph and Susan retired in town along Manor Street in Millersville.

Peeling Apples, about 1890

Wearing a checked homespun apron, Hettie Siegrist (Kreider) Miller (1835-1899) enjoys a grandchild who lived next door. Many of Hettie's grandchildren helped her with family chores. In turn, the children learned practical homemaking skills and heard Grandma's stories about earlier years.

Hettie's relative Michael Siegrist III built an imposing, stone, Georgian-styled farmhouse in West Hempfield Township in 1809 on land 1727 immigrant Michael Siegrist first settled.

About 1862, Hettie and her husband moved their young family from West Hempfield Township to Maytown. They attended Kraybill Mennonite Church.

Four Generations of Women, 1917

Relatives relax at the Ben and Alice Stauffer farm near Millersville—Fannie (Herr) Gamber, little Alta (Martin) Miller, Alice (Gamber) Stauffer, and her daughter, Hettie (Stauffer) Martin, standing.

A whitewashed fence protects garden plants from early frost. An herb garden and an orchard with cherry, apricot, apple, and peach trees produced an abundance of food for the Stauffer family.

Harnish Family, about 1910

Widower Jacob H. Harnish (1844-1935) with his six children. Jacob began embroidering quilt tops when, in his words, he was "sitting around with nothing to do and becoming an old man."

Jacob, an aging farmer from near Millersville, took up needlework in a serious way when relatives worried about him and searched for a way to have him be occupied. All efforts failed until his granddaughter embroidered a bureau scarf. She said to her grandpa, "Let's see you do this." Grandpa took the piece and, with little instruction, soon finished the border. Jacob then began making bureau scarfs, pillow covers, dresser sets, and at least seven tops for quilts.

Son Embracing His Mother, 1923

Albert Risser Leaman (1906-1979), the youngest of twelve children, with his mother Annie (Risser) Leaman (1864-1943) of Lititz. Annie's granddaughter Evelyn Huber watches nearby.

Out For a Walk, 1910

Barbara (Brenneman) Risser (1828-1924) of Lititz, mother of seven sons and one daughter. Rain or shine, summer or winter, for the young or the old—the walk to the outhouse was a necessity!

Nissley Reunion, 1917

One hundred and fifty relatives celebrate 200 years in America, 1717-1917—all descendants of Jacob and John Nissley, 1717 immigrants from Canton Berne, Switzerland, who settled in Lancaster County, Pennsylvania. The group stands by a well preserved 1774 stone homestead.

A three-column story in the July 19, 1917 local Mount Joy newspaper reported: "A very happy and unique gathering was held on Thursday, as per announcements previously sent out, at the old Nissley homestead, the Daniel E. Miller farm, one mile west of Florin, where for nearly one hundred and fifty years continuously members of the family lived. The group assembled by noon when lunch was served in sections with a liberal supply of ice cream and bananas as an embellishment. A large collection of heirlooms and souvenirs were on exhibition." The newspaper then listed the names of the one hundred fifty persons who attended.

The 1717 immigrants first settled on land that is today part of the city of Lancaster.

Walnut Grove Family Reunion, August 18, 1910

The surviving children of John Hershey Reist (1805-1877) and Marie Eby (Brubacher) Reist (1809-1887) gather with their remaining spouses. Seated from left to right: Catharine Siegrist (Garber) Reist, Sarah (Reist) Erb, Anna Brubaker (Reist) Nissly, Barbara (Reist) Snavely, Katie (Reist) Nissley, Mary E. (Peifer) Reist. Standing from left to right: John B. Reist, Jacob B. Reist, Henry Snavely, Christian Nissley.

In 1828 the parents, John H. and Marie Reist, began farming near Mount Joy. They lived in a log house west of the barn until 1833, when they built a beautiful stone house that still stands on their Walnut Grove Farm, 568 Longenecker Road. The walnut grove, planted by John, is the oldest walnut plantation in Pennsylvania.

Going Home by Honeysuckle Hill, 1916

Four young women walk near the Abram and Rebecca (Zimmerman) Diffenbach farm along the Old Philadelphia Pike and near the Mellinger Mennonite Meetinghouse along the Lincoln Highway. These are likely Diffenbach daughters with their friends. Photograph from the Diffenbach family collection.

Times Have Changed

Written about 1929 by Grace Landis Heller (1909-1934)
of Mellinger Mennonite Church, Lancaster. Used by permission of her family.

Times have changed since Grandma's day;
I can tell by the happenings she can say.
She says she walked in mud to school,
And was never allowed to loiter or fool.
She wore high-top shoes and woolen socks,
And walked around in cotton frocks.
In summer she helped the men to plow,
And in the evening milked the cow.
She helped her mother cook and bake,
Plow-lines, pies, and bread, and cake.
And when her father cradled wheat,
She took them out a nine o'clock treat.
Can't you imagine you hear them cry:
"Here comes some more good apple pie;
Come on and rest awhile now men."
Oh! It must have been great, away back then.
But times have changed since Grandma's day;
She's shocked by the happenings of today.
We usually ride to school in cars,
And sometimes loiter around for hours.
We wear slippers and pumps and silken hose,
And sometimes really all silk clothes.
Father uses a tractor now,
And I don't help to milk the cow.
We help our mothers cook and bake,
But not plow-lines for goodness sake.
We use the binder to cut the wheat,
And the men at nine o'clock don't eat.
They've just had breakfast three hours before,
And couldn't be hungry then for more.
The why or wherefore I can't say,
But times have changed since Grandma's day.

Names of Persons in Large Group Photographs

An Overview of Lancaster Mennonite Women

Page 11. Ascension Day, 1914

Seated: Man under table and boy are unidentified. Left to right: Jacob Shimp, Milton Snavely, Lloyd Huber Bomberger. Standing (left to right): Carrie Denlinger, Abe Risser, Sallie Coldren, Fannie Weidman, Ida Risser, Anne Coldren, Emma and Olivia Rupp, Alma Weidman, Helen Stauffer, Jacob Hackman. The seven persons at the end of the line are unidentified. Behind the Rupp sisters stands John Brubaker. Persons by the tree and to the right are Anna Brubaker, unidentified person, unidentified person, Annetta Erb, Maria Hackman.

Page 14. Swing in Summertime, about 1898

Front row, left to right: Anna (Herr) Brackbill, unidentified person, unidentified boy, Anna Andrews Mellinger, unidentified person, Martha, a foster girl who lived with the Mellinger family, Anna (Witmer) Brackbill, Clarence Andrews Mellinger (1890-1969). Second row, left to right: Ella (Witmer) Neff, unidentified person, Elizabeth (Mellinger) Bair, unidentified person, Esther (Kreider) Lehman, unidentified person, Anna (Baer) Eshelman, unidentified person, Ada (Kreider) Martin, Elsie (Burkey) Gochnauer Martin Ranck.

Page 22. Risser Family Reunion, 1910

A newspaper account of this May 28, 1910 event lists the Risser children and their families, but does not include a photograph that identifies them.

"The seven sons and daughter and their families follow: Christian B. Risser, wife and son Jacob, wife and child, and daughter Miss Annie, of Warwick, Jonas Hernley, wife and daughter Mrs. J. C. Paul, husband and child, of this place; Mr. Hernley's sons Henry and Christian, of Scottdale; Ivan, of Pittsburg; Albert, Elam, Jacob, Melvin, Lloyd, at home. Maggie and husband John Bucher, of Clay, and daughter Mrs. Chas. Musser and husband, of Lansdown; a daughter Ella, also of Lansdown, and son Abram and daughter Anna. Annie and husband N.B. Leaman, of this place, and daughter Mrs. Martin Moore, husband and two children of Mt. Joy; a son, C.K. Leaman, wife and child; sons and daughters, Martha, Kathryn, Henry, Grace, Frank, Paul, Esther, Ruth, and Albert. Jacob Risser, wife and sons and daughters, Harry, Lizzie, Victor, Ella, Susan, Annie, and J. Hershey Risser, of Brunnerville. Elam, wife and children Anna, Martin, Miriam. Miss Elizabeth Risser, who resides with her mother.

"There were only three of the kin who were unable to attend. Mrs. Leaman's niece, Victor Breneman and wife, of Harrisburg, were also present."

Page 23. Hayride from Strasburg, 1904

Left to right: Nettie (Landis) Myer, Lizzie (Musser) Redcay, Annie (Landis) Rohrer, Clara (Landis) Landis, Fannie (Diffenbach) Rohrer, Amelia (Witmer) Groff, Lydia (Landis) Landis, Gertrude (Cooper) Poole, Katie (Denlinger) Landis, Lizzie (Groff) Sweigart, Cora

Esbenshade, Lydia (Ranck) Herr, Edna Heller, Stella (Landis) Heller, Bertha Rohrer, and Frances Esbenshade.

Page 27. A Wedding Portrait, 1899

As newlyweds, Elam and Mattie (Keener) Burkhart moved into a new home built on the Samuel Huber Burkhart farm along the Old Philadelphia Pike near Bridgeport. There they reared four children, tended thirteen greenhouses, and went to market.

Mennonites and Early Photography

Page 40. Girl Crowd, 1915

Left to right, first row: Hannah Wissler, Anna Longenecker, Emma Weist, Mae Brenner, Amelia Buckwalter, Minnie Rudy, Susan Hershey, Alma Risser, Elva Risser. Second row: Elva Wissler, Anna Brubaker, Mary Bucher, Fanny Weist, Cora Landis, Gertrude Reifsnyder, Ida Brubaker, Salina Brubaker, Anna Erb, Nora Bucher. Third row (standing): unidentified person, Bertha Stauffer, Elva Brubaker, Elizabeth Landis, Anna Becker, Ada Peiffer, Carrie Zwally, Alice Stauffer, Katie Bollinger, Barbara Bollinger, Fannie Brubaker, Emma Erb, Alma Weidman. Fourth row: Howard Hess, John Brubaker, Lizzie Bomberger, Ada Hershey, Nora Longenecker, Maria Hackman, Ida Risser.

Page 41. New Holland Youth, about 1920

According to Mary (Weaver) Harsh (1902-1994), photographer, the specific order of persons is unknown, but is approximately this: Seated (left to right): unidentified person, Hettie (Martin) Rupert, Lydia Weaver, Isaac Buckwalter. Standing (left to right): Mahlon Rutt, Elizabeth Rutt, unidentified person, Elsie (Hershey) Mellinger, John Rutt, Violet Rutt.

"Running Around"

Page 46. Charles Cousins, about 1873

Left to right: Mary G. Charles, John F. Charles, Mary H. Charles, Levi F. Charles, Christian F. Charles, Lizzie H. Charles, Catherine G. (Kate) Charles, Henry H. Charles, Emma F. Charles, David F. Charles, Abraham F. Charles, Christiana F. Charles.

Page 56. Ocean Grove, about 1918

Nora Hershey, Hettie (Hoober) Nolt, Elsie (Hershey) Mellinger, and Ada of Farmersville pose in their swimwear. The particular identity of each person remains uncertain.

Page 57. Hotel Waitresses at Ocean Grove, 1915

Left to right: Martha (Garber) Miller, Anna (Mummau) Drescher, Mary (Brubaker) Weaver, unidentified person, Maude (Strickler) Gainer, Mary (Strickler) Longenecker, Jane (Strickler) Rohrer, Ellen Garber, Mary (Mummau) Rohrer, Susie (Garber) Musser, Mary (Stauffer) Garber, unidentified person.

Page 62. Sunday Afternoon, 1914

Left to right, front row: Martha Steinman, Blanche Erb, Helen (Snavely) Hess, Vera Harvey, Grena Moore, Elsie Erb. Back Row: Margaret Lantz, Anna Musser, Anna Heller, unidentified person.

Page 64. Ephrata and Weaverland Girl Crowd, 1920's

Left to right, front row: Anna Mary (Sauder) Martin, Mabel (Weaver) Marner, Amanda (Geigley) Heller, Anna (Martin) Martin Zimmerman, Esther (Landis) Minnich, Helen (Mellinger) Weaver, Lizzie (Sauder) Ebersole, Dora (Sauder) Horning, Grace Mosemann, Naomi (Burkholder) Boll, Minnie (Sauder) Weaver. Second row: Martha Snyder, Elva (Huber) Wenger, Anna (Horst) Wolf Herr, Verna Zimmerman, Ada (Horst) Weaver, Mary (Wissler) Byer, Lydia (Hurst) Wenger, Ada Zimmerman Brunk, Eva (Burkholder) Tyson, Martha (Nolt) Martin, Katie (Horst) Shenk. Third row: Erel Mosemann, Esther (Sauder) Reist, Fannie Weidman, Mary Geigley, Etta (Martin) Weaver, Mary Sauder, Mary (Martin) Zimmerman, Esther Mellinger Bair, Vera (Oberholtzer) Dillman, Esther Beck, Esther (Sensenig) Fisher, Alma Snyder, Minnie (Eberly) Holsopple Good, Ellen Martin, Anna (Snavely) Weidman, Esther (Burkholder) Weaver, Martha (Martin) Snyder, Eva (Burkholder) Clark, Anna Good Becker.

Hostess: Leah (Martin) Sauder.

Page 66. A Mennonite Girl Crowd in Lititz, 1914

Left to right, front row: Ada Peifer, Mary Bucher, Hannah Wissler, Emma Erb, Anna Mumaw, Bertha Stauffer, Anna Mae (Erb) Huber, Anna (Brubaker) Keller, Esther Hersh, Anna Becker. Second row: unidentified person, unidentified person, Marie Habecker, Ella (Landis) Breneman, Alice Becker, Bertha Bucher, Alice Stauffer. Third row: Agnes Klein, Anna (Erb) Hess, Martha (Eby) Yake, Martha (Leaman) Rudy, Kathryn (Hersh) Longenecker, Eva Royer, Kathryn Royer, Grace Hershey, Elsie (Bucher) Groff, Fannie (Brubaker) Erb Landis, Amy Heagy. Fourth row: Lizzie (Landis) Bomberger, Lizzie Mumaw, Elizabeth Royer, Kathryn (Leaman) Swarr, hostess Anna (Snyder) Erb, Elva Wissler, Lizzie Bomberger.

Motherhood and Children

Page 83. Rutt Family, about 1910

Seated on the lawn, left to right: Viola W. Rutt, Elizabeth (Rutt) Horst. Second row: Anna (Rutt) Sauder, Clara (Rutt) Buchen, mother Elizabeth Rutt holding Marian, father Aaron B. Rutt, Clarence Henry Rutt, Katie W. Rutt. Third row: Phares W. Rutt, Mary (Rutt) Weaver, Susan W. Rutt.

Farm Life and Work

Page 116. Barn Raising Cooks, 1909

First row, left to right: Arthur Swarr, unidentified person, unidentified person, unidentified person, unidentified person. Second row: Frances (Bear) Keener, Ada (Newcomer) Garber, Lillie (Stauffer) Landis, Bertha (Hertzler) Bucher holding Irene, unidentified person, unidentified person, Alice (Emsweiler) Flory, unidentified person. Third row: Barbara (Fry) Reist, Katie (Strickler)

Herr, Charlotte (Hertzler) Heistand, unidentified person, Lizzie (Snavely) Heisey, unidentified person, Sadie (Hertzler) Flinchbach. Fourth row: Fianna (Nissley) Reist, Martha (Hershey) Fry, Mrs. Hiram Strickler, Sr., hostess Charlotte (Nissley) Hertzler [hidden], Emma (Nissley) Bear, Sadie (Nissley) Swarr, Adeline Hertzler, Anna (Flory) Eby, Mary (Rohrer) Nissley [step-mother to hostess], unidentified person.

Page 117. Waitresses for a Barn Raising Meal, 1892

Adults seated left to right: Frances Engle, Annie Charles, unidentified Hottenstein, Annie (Strickler) Newcomer, unidentified Charles, Elmira (Nissley) Nissley, Fannie Harnish. Children: Mary Charles, Annie Charles, Ray Engle, unidentified Brenneman child. Standing: Esther Charles, unidentified Newcomer, Barbara (Newcomer) Longenecker, Lizzie Newcomer, Annie Lindemuth, unidentified Lindemuth, Barbara (Nissley) Miller, Lizzie Haverstick.

Church Life and Faith

Page 147. Wedding Portrait, 1900

As a young woman Anna May graduated from Millersville Normal School. In the 1920s, after eight children, she began classes at Eastern Mennonite School (now Eastern Mennonite University) where A. D. Wenger, her husband, was president from 1922-1935. About 1935 she graduated with a degree in elementary Bible. See *Pennsylvania Mennonite Heritage,* April 1981, for more details on the evangelism movement that greatly involved the Wenger household and many other Mennonite families in Lancaster County.

Page 149. Rock Point School, 1893

Front row, left to right: Ida Saylor, Virgie Deitz, John Otto, John Myers, Park Zalm, Jacob Baker. Second row: Sadie Myers, Grace Deitz, Anna Nissly, Mazzie Hawthorne, John Deitz, John Mumma, Enos Gibble. Third row: Minnie Saylor, Emma Baker, Sarah Habecker, Katie Ottean, Elmer Myers, Harry Spicer, Paris Hawthorne, Harry Saylor. Fourth row: Abram Longenecker, teacher, Katie Nissly, Mazzie Brandt, Bessie Mumma, Amanda Boyer, Otto Neigeth, Clyde Yundish, unidentified person, unidentified person. Back row: Bertha Deitz, Fannie Eyer, Linden Flory, Lizzie Nissly, Jacob Saylor, Irvin Lindemuth, Benjamin Hawthorne, John Witmer, Harvy Hawthorne.

Page 155. Rohrer and Landis Gathering, 1911

Seated, left to right: Margaret (Gremli) Rohrer, Ruth Zimmerman, who later married the photographer Landis Rohrer, Lizzie (Diffenbach) Martin, Bertha (Wenger) Rohrer, Peter L. Rohrer, Cora (Sauder) Sauder, Blanche (Mowrer) Shenk, Nettie (Landis) Myer. Standing: John L. Rohrer, Ira Myers, unidentified person, Benjamin Rohrer, Clarence Shenk, John N. Sauder. The two children belong to workers at the Glick Plant Farm.

The Lure of the West

Page 185. Daughter with Elderly Mother, 1900
Some descendants of "Tennessee John" and Catharine Stoltzfus who were significant Christian leaders or educators: Daniel Hertzler, former editor of *Gospel Herald;* Mae Hertzler Hershey, lifelong missionary in Argentina; Lester Hershey, lifelong missionary in Puerto Rico; Beatrice Hershey Hallman, missionary in Argentina; Mary M. Good, educator in India mission schools; Crissie Yoder Shank, missionary to India; Mary and Katherine Royer, teachers and writers in Christian education; Elizabeth Royer Neff, educator; and Christina Neff Okamoto, namesake of her grandmother and an active educator.

Page 187. Farewell to Relatives, 1909
Left to right: Alice Shaubach, Henry Rohrer, Parke Shaubach, Mary Mellinger, Edith Stoner (with black coat), Elias Mellinger, stepmother Isabel Stoner, Edith Mellinger (littlest girl in big hat and cousin to Edith and Anna Stoner). In back are Ida Mellinger, Anna Stoner (youth in big hat), and Ella Rohrer.

Page 188. Western and Eastern Relatives, 1917
Kneeling, left to right: John Charles, David Hess, Naomi Hess, Irvin Charles, Anna Charles, Mary Hess, Stanley Charles. Middle: David F. Charles, Anna (Mellinger) Charles, Maria (Neff) Mellinger, Amelia (Charles) Charles. Back: teacher/preacher John Denlinger Charles, preacher Jacob Hess holding Edward, and Katie (Charles) Hess.

Anna Charles, center front, started to dress plain as a nine-year-old in 1917. During one of the first revival services held by the Kansas Mennonites, she stood to become a Christian. In 1995 at age eighty-seven, Anna said, "Afterwards my parents blessed me for my decision. During my youth, Father became a revivalist to the Texas panhandle and as far north as Canada during the summer when he was not teaching science at Hesston College. Our family all pulled together for church growth and college success. After father's early death at forty-five years old, we moved back to Pennsylvania so that relatives could help Mother with us children."

Quilting and the Arts

Page 203. ABC Circle, 1923
Seated, left to right: Barbara (Nissley) Miller, Myra (Gamber) Good, Elverta Bair, Mary (Metzler) Frey, Mary (Hershey) Kreider. Second row: Irene (Brubaker) Landis, Mary Shearer, Mary (Heller) Landis, Pauline Stroebel. Back row: Anna Mae (Greider) Grove, Sarah (Root) Landis, and Fanny (Root) Forry. Susan (Shearer) Landis and Anna (Buckwalter) Hoober, members of the circle, were not in this photograph.

Older Years and Reunions

Page 210. Harnish Family, about 1910
The children, left to right, are: Fannie, Emma, Ada, Enos, Lizzie, and Annie.

References and Resources

Benner, Henry, ed. *The Story of the Paradise Mennonite Church.* Paradise, PA, 1985.

Eby, Martin C. *Family and Descendants of H. John and Sarah Eby.* Kinzers, PA, 1976.

Eby, Martin C. *The History of the Hershey Mennonite Church.* Kinzers, PA, 1978.

Gehret, Ellen J. *Rural Pennsylvania Clothing.* York, PA: Liberty Cap Books, 1976.

Hess Family. *The Fruitful Vine, The Hess Family of Pequea.* New Danville, PA, 1981.

Hess, John H. *Hess Genealogy.* Lititz, PA, 1896.

Kauffman, *John E. Anabaptist Letters 1635-1645, translated from the Ausbund.* Atglen, PA, 1977.

Landis Family. *Bicentennial of First Landis Settlement in Lancaster County and Seventh Annual Landis Family Reunion.* Lititz, PA, 1917.

Nissly Family. *Levi R. and Lizzie L. Nissly.* Mount Joy, PA, 1975.

Reist Family. *Family Record of Jacob B. Reist and Mary Peifer Reist of Lancaster County Pennsylvania.* Gordonville, PA, 1979.

Reist, Henry G. *Peter Reist of Lancaster County, Pennsylvania and Some of His Descendants.* Schenectady, NY, 1933.

Roupp, Paul E. and Gertrude. *Roots Continuing Generations of John Risser Hess, 1828-1897.* Hesston, KS, 1980.

Genealogical files and Library of the Lancaster Mennonite Historical Society, Lancaster, PA.

Pennsylvania Mennonite Heritage, a quarterly magazine published by the Lancaster Mennonite Historical Society, Lancaster, PA. April, 1981, October, 1982, and April, 1988 issues.

From Great-Great-Great-Grandmother to the Author

Upper row, left to right: Barbara Schock Ziegler (1793-1879) married Jacob Wolf Lindemuth on March 4, 1817. Barbara Ziegler Lindemuth (1825-1899) married Christian Hershey Nissly about 1845. Lizzie Lindemuth Nissly (1854-1932) married Levi Reist Nissly on October 25, 1871. Lower row, left to right: Anna Nissly Nissly (1885-1947) married John Bomberger Nissley on November 1, 1906. Kathryn Nissly Nissley (born September 22, 1921) married David Leaman Hess, Jr., on May 15, 1943. Her daughter, Joanne (Hess) Siegrist is the author of this book.

About the Author

Joanne Hess Siegrist, a tenth generation Pennsylvanian, grew up on her family's farm in Lancaster County. She holds a B.S. in Home Economics and has worked in social services and as a secondary schoolteacher. In recent years she has initiated educational efforts through presentations and publications related to church, family life, and heritage themes.

Siegrist served as historian for the Stumptown Mennonite Church from 1986-1992, and as photographic editor for *Bomberger Lancaster County Roots, 1722-1986; Through the Years with Fanny, 1906-1989; Locust Grove Mennonite School 1939-1989;* and *Passing on the Faith: The Story of a Mennonite School, 1942-1992.* In 1991 and 1993 she helped direct an Antique Quilt and Photography Exhibit for Lancaster Mennonite High School. In 1993 Siegrist became photography harvest coordinator for Lancaster Mennonite Historical Society.

A parent of three sons, she and her husband, J. Donald Siegrist, M.D., live in Bird-In-Hand, Pennsylvania.

220